"These once and future stories are so masterfully told, so richly embroidered, and so deeply felt that they call up in the reader a bittersweet remembrance of the *pathos* and possibilities of love. Diane Wolkstein is surely one of the great storytellers of the twentieth century and what she brings to this most ancient of all arts is a deep understanding of the ways of the heart matched with exquisite craftsmanship and unmatchable passion for and skill with language."

—Jean Huston, Ph.D.
Author of *The Search for the Beloved*

"These are powerful, haunting love stories. For Diane is a true storyteller. She knows there is no need to hurry the telling and, still, the stories end too soon. She finds a new voice for each retelling, rhythms and language that seem perfectly fitted to the vision they embody. She retells with intelligence, with respect, with delight—and love."

—Christine Downing
Professor of Religious Studies
San Diego State University

"A splendid collection of indispensable tales of love, handsomely retold by that rarity in our time, a true teller of tales. Engrossing and entertaining."

—Barry Ulanov
Professor Emeritus of Literature
Barnard College

"In *The First Love Stories* Diane Wolkstein tells us about desire, sensuality, passion and all the myths that have embodied them since the beginning of time. It is creation itself we experience as we read her book, and as a bonus, we are swept along by the very emotions which for the last six millennia have made life worth living."

—Olivier Bernier
Lecturer, Metropolitan Museum of Art

ALSO BY DIANE WOLKSTEIN

Inanna, Queen of Heaven and Earth,
Her Stories and Hymns from Sumer
(with S. N. Kramer)

Abulafia: Part of My Heart

Dreamsongs

The Legend of Sleepy Hollow

Oom Razoom: Go I Know Not Where,
Bring Back I Know Not What

Owl

The Banza

The Magic Wings

White Wave

The Magic Orange Tree and Other Haitian Folktales

The Red Lion

The Visit

Squirrel's Song

Lazy Stories

The Cool Ride in the Sky

8,000 Stones

THE FIRST LOVE STORIES

FROM ISIS AND OSIRIS TO TRISTAN AND ISEULT

DIANE WOLKSTEIN

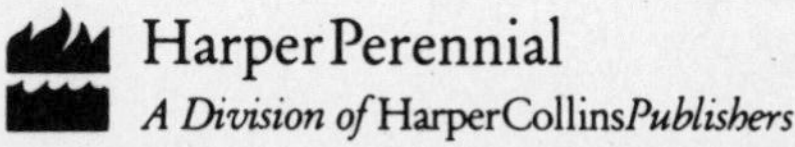
HarperPerennial
A Division of HarperCollins*Publishers*

A hardcover edition of this book was published in 1991 by HarperCollins Publishers.

First HarperPerennial edition published 1992.

Designed by Karen Savary

The Library of Congress has catalogued the hardcover edition as follows:

Wolkstein, Diane.
The first love stories: from Isis and Osiris to Tristan and Iseult/Diane Wolkstein.—1st ed.
p. cm.
Contents: Isis and Osiris—Inanna and Dumuzi—Shiva and Sati—The Song of Songs—Psyche and Eros—Layla and Majnun—Tristan and Iseult.
ISBN 0-06-016220-1
1. Love stories. 2. Mythology. 3. Folklore. I. Title.
PN6071.L7W65 1991
808.8'0354—dc20 90-55558

ISBN 0-06-092272-9 (pbk.)
96 CC/RRD 10 9

October 21, 1999

For lovers everywhere

For Philip and Chantal,

Stories for lovers

to read aloud

together.

Lovely to meet

both of you..

Diane.

CONTENTS

INTRODUCTION

Thwack! The arrow of the great archer, Kama, hits its mark. *Thwack!* Struck by curiosity, Psyche wounds herself with Eros' arrow. Once there was a time before love; then, love begins. . . .

On the morning of February 6, 1977, it was still snowing. It had been snowing for nearly forty hours. The subways had stopped. The theatres uptown were closed. Despite the snow-storm we decided to go on anyhow. This would be the first performance of a series called Winter Tales by Candlelight.

It was wonderful walking to the theater. Not one car was on the street. It was perfectly quiet: snow was everywhere. When I arrived at the Theatre of the Open Eye in Greenwich Village, sixty people were already there, rosy and glowing with snow glitters on their cheeks. They were hardy and excited. A few were friends; most were people I did not know.

For years I had been preparing for this event. It was the culmination of a dream: stories for adults.

I began with the Sephardic story "Moses and the Water Carrier." The penniless water carrier pleads with Moses to ask God to change the lines on his forehead so his fate may be changed. Moses forgets. But God admonishes him: "Moses, isn't there something you're forgetting to ask me?" Moses asks, and the water carrier's fate is changed. The night before, the water carrier had only the earth for his bed and the sky for his blanket; the night after, he became the son-in-law of the wealthiest merchant in the village.

The second story was the Sufi tale "The Red Lion," in which the prince runs away three times from three different lions until he realizes that wherever he goes, there will always be a lion waiting for him, unless he confronts his own fears.

It was the last story, "Layla and Majnun," which was an hour and a half long, on which the series depended. Would adults care to listen for an hour and a half to a story of passion?

I began. My fears left me, and only the story was present. The audience reached out and took each word and bore it up. No one coughed, or sighed, or moved, until it was over. The story sang. The audience listened with such intensity and feeling that I felt as if we were flying together through the desert sky.

In the middle of the night, the words of "Layla and Majnun" returned to me. They woke me up. And I spoke Majnun's words again:

"Oh God, let me not be cured of love, but let my passion grow! Let me love for love's sake! Take what is left of my life and give it to Layla! Make my love a hundred times greater than it is today!"

At last I fell asleep. A few hours later I was awakened by my daughter; time for first grade. Walking Rachel to school, holding her small hand, I was filled with great peace and happiness. The sun was shining. We were not walking on cement; we were walking on heaven's offering, three to four feet of snow.

I told her about the evening. She had already heard the story at the dress rehearsal the night before. She asked, "How long does it take to be ten?" (I had told her she could come to the winter tales when she was ten years old.)

"Five years," I answered.

"I want to be ten tomorrow."

"I'll tell you my favorite part of the story again," I said, and we stood on a snowbank on the corner of Greenwich Avenue and West 10th Street and I proclaimed for Rachel, for the morning, for the snow, for life:

Let me not be cured of love, but let my passion grow! Make my love a hundred times greater than it is today! And let me love for love's sake!

So the stories for love's sake began. First in performance, then research, then performance, then more research, writing, and rewriting, for fourteen years. My daughter wanted to be older. I wanted to be wiser.

Each story had its own method and journey. "Isis and Osiris" involved years of detailed research in many libraries, enlivened by my journey down the Nile to Hathor's temple at Dendera, Osiris' temple at Abydos, Horus' temple at Edfu, and Isis' temple at Philae.

"Inanna and Dumuzi" found its shape after more than 100 performances throughout the United States and Europe.

The story of "Shiva and Sati" came to me in a vision and a phone call. In 1978, I was preparing to tell a part of "The Mabinogion" at the New School for Social Research in New York City. My mind kept drifting. I couldn't picture Rhiannon. Instead, I kept seeing a slender, young woman of great energy with swinging, dark hair sitting at the back of the New School auditorium. I called Joseph Campbell to ask him a question about "The Mabinogion." He said the answer was in *The King and the*

Corpse. When I took out the book, it opened to "Four Romances of the Goddess," a story of Shiva and Sati, in which Sati's father meditated on the nature of the great Maya until "the goddess at last bodily appeared to him, dark and slender, with her hair hanging free." I chose to tell their story instead.

Work on "The Song of Songs" was intense and joyous. In defending the entry of "The Song of Songs" into the canon, Rabbi Akiva said that the world is not worth the day "The Song of Songs" was created. The Hebrew scholar, Ray Scheindlin, who first translated the verses for me, knew it by heart and insisted that the only correct way to translate it was to recite the lines in Hebrew aloud. He lingered over the sounds, repeating the Hebrew with delight whenever the sound was the sense. In reciting the words to twentieth-century audiences, I tried to find the right tone for each word and the right melody for each line. My most concentrated work was in rehearsal and performance. I performed "The Song of Songs" at universities, museums, and weddings. When I performed it well, I felt as if I were wearing a shining transparent cloth, which let the wind pass through freely.

In 1982 I began work on a literal translation of "Psyche and Eros" from the Latin of Apuleius' *The Golden Ass.* For three years I worked alone at the translating. In 1983, I visited the sites of the Greek gods and goddesses, including the Oracle of Apollo at Miletus. Because of the wit and style of Apuleius, I chose to spend more time translating and writing than performing.

As for "Layla and Majnun," I rarely performed the story; my emotion was spent in the reading and writing of it. In his afterword to "Layla and Majnun," Peter Chelkowski writes that the author, Nizami, must have been in a trance when he composed it, for he wrote over 2,000 rhyming lines within four months. I completed most of the rewriting in the fall of 1987, a time of great personal grief and sadness. I wept as I worked on it, but somehow whenever I worked on it, my grief was lifted.

"Tristan and Iseult" was the slowest to complete. During the summer and fall of 1986, I wove the story together from five different strands. Audiences preferred "Tristan and Iseult" to everything I had previously done; I found it draining and exhausting. During the years I worked on it, I had four car accidents. Each time I recovered, another vehicle hit me from behind.

At last, I began to work with Richard Armstrong from the Roy Hart Theatre. In rehearsal, I would continuously groan and sigh. After two weeks of this, Richard said, "Diane, can you put those groans and sighs into words?" *"What? This dark, miserable story!"* I said. Out came the fool's comments—and the storyteller was free to tell the story she believed in.

In each story in this collection, a transformation occurs—often unexpected. Each story expresses a different aspect of love: love greater than nature ("Isis and Osiris"), love between father and son and the creating of the soul ("Layla and Majnun"), love of community vs. love of self ("Tristan and Iseult"), the explosion of passion and the taming of the mind ("Shiva and Sati"), the cyclic aspect of love ("Inanna and Dumuzi"), the sensuous, celebratory, yearning quality of love ("The Song of Songs"), the forging of the self ("Psyche and Eros"). It depends where you are on your life journey which story will be strongest for you.

These stories are mysteries. Rooted in creation, separation, and rebirth, the slow process each one demanded for its shaping could not be hastened. Yet, as the years passed, these stories, from completely diverse cultures, nourished, inspired, and comforted me. Like indescribable landscapes and ecstatic music, they have given me joy. I think of the first lines of "The Song of Songs":

Let him kiss me with the kisses of your mouth,
for your love is more wonderful than wine. . . .

Different pronouns? Yes, different pronouns to celebrate the different forms of love, the personal and the divine. Whatever the culture, the stories join the soul to itself and to a larger inspiration of life.

With good reason, love's messengers, Eros and Kama, are armed with bows and long-distance arrows. No being, god or mortal, can choose love. Love comes despite ourselves; and then, if we have not already done so, we have the task of becoming our selves so we may welcome love.

The night that I first told "Layla and Majnun," I also told the Jewish story of the penniless water carrier who dared to ask and the Arabic story of the prince who dared to face his fears. Both are needed: the asking and the daring to face one's fears.

As a young man, Majnun asked: "Make my love a hundred times greater than it is today!" And then he continued to brave his fears, the little ones and the big ones, so that after loving Layla all his life, he could say: "Love is my fire and essence. The bundle which is my self is gone. Love has entered my house. You do not see me. You see 'the beloved.' How then can love be torn from my heart?"

Majnun received love, not the passion he had specifically imagined, but a greater love—compassion.

I am grateful to the poets whose life-blood created these stories. Let Eros draw his bow. Let Kama's arrow fly.

Once there was a time before love; then, love begins. . . .

ISIS AND OSIRIS

The Sunboat of a Million Years

For Nina Singer

Hail Atum! You shine at dusk!
Hail Khepri! You shine at dawn!
Hail Re! You shine at noon!
You are the First Hill!
You give birth to yourself!

In the primeval waters, Atum, the One, came into being. He lay in the dark waters listless and weary. Then his heart was stirred to create all kinds of beings. He deliberated in his mind. He entered his heart and the plan of the universe rose before him.

Atum, the great He-She, joined with himself. He rubbed his phallus with his fist. He spat out from his mouth. Out came a son—air, and a daughter—moisture. Atum held his children in his embrace, imparting to them his ka, his life force. For a time, his children rejoiced in the Nun, the dark waters. Then they disappeared.

Atum sent his Eye to find his children. For years, she searched for them. Then another Eye grew in Atum's forehead. At last, the first Eye returned with the children. Atum rejoiced to be with them again. He named his son Shu, meaning life, and his daughter Tefnut, meaning order. In his gladness he wept, and from his tears the first men and women sprang into being. Then his heart was stirred again and he yearned to find a place to rest himself.

Nun, the dark waters, spoke to him and said, "Kiss your daughter, so your heart may be strengthened. Do not let Tefnut leave you, for she is order. Do not let Shu leave you, for he is life. Let your son and daughter, life and order, remain together." With his breath, Shu raised Atum up. Atum kissed Tefnut. As he did so, he emerged from the waters in the form of the First Hill; the first light shone in the world.

When Atum's first Eye saw that Atum had grown a brighter, more radiant eye in her place, she was furious. She changed herself into a roaring cobra with a swollen neck. To appease her jealous wrath, Atum set her in the center of his forehead. There, in her wisdom, power, and blazing light, she became the Lady of the Crown.

Atum's children, Shu and Tefnut, air and water, joined together and gave birth to Geb and Nut, the earth and the sky. The earth and the sky gave birth to Osiris, Seth, Isis, and Nephthys. From these gods, all the multitudes of gods which form the world came into being.

Geb gave to his firstborn son, Osiris, the black fertile land, the water, the plants, the cattle, and all the birds of the sky. To his younger son, Seth, he gave the storm, the winds, and the desert. In those early days, bandits roamed everywhere causing strife and hunger. Osiris overthrew the bandits and brought order to the land. He allowed the son to take the father's place. He taught the people to plant barley and emmer. He taught them to honor and respect the gods. Atum in the form of the sun god Re gave Osiris the kingship. Thoth, the god of justice, crowned Osiris with the Double Crown of the Two Lands.

Osiris married Isis. When there was peace and abundance in the land, he entrusted Isis with the kingship and set out with a small band of musicians and priests to explore other countries. He hunted. He fought. He built cities. Everywhere he went he taught people to grow plants. He charmed the people with his voice and his songs, and in return, they gave him wonderful gifts. All of these—ivory, gold, animals, jewels—he sent home to Isis.

In Egypt, Osiris' younger brother, Seth, wanted to take the throne from Isis and many times he tried with guile to seduce her. But Isis' heart and mind were clear and she always understood Seth's intentions. As the gifts from other countries arrived, Isis began to long for the return of her husband. She had the court painter paint her portrait and sent it as a gift to Osiris. When he received her portrait, he wrote to her at once:

"Dearest one, sister without peer,
when I gaze at you,
I see my heart's desire
shining before me
like the rising morning star
on the first day of the New Year.

Your hair glitters like lapis
your eyes are radiant
your nipples alluring
your arms like burnished gold
your fingers as delicate as lotus blossoms.

How firm are your thighs. How slender your waist.
How the men must turn their heads,
longingly, as you pass.
Fortune belongs to the man who can please you.
I will return soon, my dearest one."

Isis wrote back to Osiris:

"When I think of you, my heart flutters.
I can not act sensibly anymore.
My heart leaps from its place—
I do not know which dress to put on
I can scarcely fasten my shawl
I forget to put on my eye-paint—

Come quickly, my brother,
too many months have passed."

Osiris:

"My sister, I am riding north in the ferry.
I carry plants and roots.
The oarsmen dip their reeds in the water,
and the river pulls like wine."

Isis:

"My eyes are fixed on the garden gate.
My ears are straining.
I am waiting for you who neglected me.
I watch the road;
my heart no longer silent.

Come quickly, my brother,
like a gazelle fleeing in the wild,
its feet reeling, its limbs weary,
leaping from hill to hill, trembling
from fear of the hunter."

Osiris:

"Isis has cast her net,
and ensnared me

in the noose of her hair.
I am held by her eyes
curbed by her necklace
imprisoned in the scent of her skin."

Isis:

"My brother, you hold me in your arms
and I do as you wish.
My longing for you is my eye-paint.
I press closer to you so I may gaze at you,
O let this hour go on forever.

The smell of your breath stirs my heart.
You bring me sorrow and joy;
do not leave me.

I belong to you, my brother, like this black earth
growing with flowers and sweet-smelling herbs.
My melilote flower, your plants summon us.
The stream you dug with your own hand
flows by our side.
The north wind refreshes us.
How lovely it is to wander hand in hand.

The sound of your voice is pomegranate wine.
I live by hearing it.
Your looks—each look—sustain me
more than food or drink."

Osiris:

"My sister, my wife, my favorite,
I open my arms to hold you.
I kiss you—your lips open.

My arms bound like a red fish in a pond.
O night, be mine forever
now that Isis is in my arms."

And so it was that Osiris returned to Egypt. With his coming, the waters of the Nile rose higher than they had in many years. There was peace and abundance. There were festivals and celebrations. The people adored Osiris.

Seth despised him. He plotted against the brother who had been given everything. He brooded until he thought of a way to destroy the happiness of Osiris and Isis.

Seth was married to Isis' sister, Nephthys, who resembled Isis in many ways. The two sisters often exchanged visits. Seth had fine linen robes woven for Nephthys that were identical to the ones that Isis wore. He braided his wife's hair to match Isis' hairstyle. He praised Nephthys, saying, "Every day, you grow more like your radiant sister, Isis." And the timid Nephthys, innocent of Seth's intentions, was pleased.

One evening at dusk, when Nephthys was in Isis' garden, Osiris came up behind her and, thinking that she was Isis, put one hand around her slender waist and fondled her bare breast with his other hand. Nephthys cried out in fright. But Osiris, thinking she was delighted, lifted her into the air and carried her protesting to their secret place in the garden. As the wild goose shrilled, Osiris covered her mouth with kisses, saying, "Delicious woman, you draw me to you. How can I resist? My sister, my wife, my favorite!"

Nephthys became pregnant. She did not dare tell Seth. She hid her pregnancy, telling only her servant and feigning illness. When the child was born, she and her servant took him far from the city and laid him to die in a bed of melilote flowers.

Isis was gathering herbs by the Nile when Nephthys' servant

came up to her and asked permission to speak. The servant told her how Osiris had mistakenly consorted with her sister and that the child from that one meeting lay exposed at this moment in the wilderness. Isis called her dogs and went at once in the direction the girl had described. She heard the child's muffled cries and soon found the infant among the rocks, wrapped in royal linen, lying in a bed of melilote flowers. Isis brought the child back to the palace. She named him Anubis and raised him to be her guardian and attendant. She did not speak of the child's birth to either Nephthys or Osiris. After waiting so many months for his return, she did not want anything to disturb the love between herself and her husband.

Seth watched the love between Isis and Osiris deepen and his rage grew. Not only did Isis adore her husband, but whenever Osiris appeared on the streets, the people hailed him and cried with joy. Seth continued to brood, and in time he discovered there were other men in the kingdom who were also jealous of Osiris' power and fame. Seth mingled with them and carefully gathered together a group of seventy-two conspirators. Aso, the queen of Ethiopia, a powerful and treacherous sorceress, who was visiting Seth, found out the measurements of Osiris' body and gave them to Seth. Seth then had a wooden chest made which fit the measurements of Osiris exactly. The chest was decorated with ivory, ebony, carnelian, lapis, and gold.

In the month that the sun passes through Scorpio, when all was in readiness, Seth held a banquet in Osiris' honor. The carefree Osiris had no suspicions and arrived without guards or attendants. Osiris was gay and easy. He sang for the guests. Throughout the dinner, adoring and amusing toasts were offered to Osiris. Musicians accompanied him on the lute and drums. Dinner was sumptuous. Fish, fowl, salads, cheese, grapes, dates, melons, and every kind of bread were served.

After dinner, before the games began, Seth removed a fine linen cloth from a chest that was lying in the center of the room. Everyone admired the chest. Then Seth opened it and it was even more beautiful inside than out. It was a perfect coffin.

"I shall give this coffin to whomever it fits," Seth announced. One guest after another eagerly laid down in the coffin. It was larger than all the men who were present. Then Osiris laid down in the coffin. It fit him perfectly.

"The coffin belongs to Osiris!" Seth shouted and rang a bell which was a signal to the conspirators. They ran to the chest and pushed down the lid. Osiris cried out and pushed against the lid. The men worked feverishly hammering nails into the coffin until it was shut.

With Osiris' cries in their ears, the men carried the coffin north for three days and three nights until they came to the mouth of the Tanitic River. There, at dawn, they placed the chest in the sea and as it floated away they gave their final toasts: "Hail Osiris! Son of Geb! Hail Osiris! Son of Nut! Lord of Abundance! Where is your power now? Where is your double-horned crown?"

When they could no longer see the chest, they stopped their toasts and hurried to their homes. Seth was content. Now he would rule Egypt.

When Isis learned of her husband's death, she wept. She tore her clothes. She covered her hair with dust. She put on mourning clothes. She cried out:

"Heaven weeps!
Earth trembles at this deed!
Re is in the heavens and yet it is dark.
The heavens and earth are one.
The earth is in shadow.

My tears flood the land.
They burn my face.
Do not forsake me, Osiris.
Come to your sister.
Take away the pain in my body.
You who never found fault with me.
Do not leave me.

Heaven has fallen through to earth.
I walk the roads searching for you.
Fire burns in my heart.
I grieve that you are alone.
I stretch out my arms to greet you."

Isis went in search of Osiris. She wandered over the Delta, asking everyone she met, even the children, if they had seen her husband's casket. Then three children, who had been playing at dawn near the Tanitic River, told her that they had seen a large group of men whispering together and carrying a shining box to the edge of the river and shouting, "Hail Osiris! Son of Geb! Hail Osiris! Son of Nut!" The children told her that they had crept to the river's edge and watched as the golden box had floated out to sea.

Many months later, Isis learned that the coffin had been found in Byblos. The waves had thrust it into the trunk of a tamarisk tree. The bark had enfolded the casket and the tree had continued to grow. When the king of Byblos heard of this marvel, he visited the tree. He admired the width of the tree and ordered it to be cut down and the section containing the casket to be carved into a pillar to support the palace.

Isis crossed the sea to Byblos. Before she went to the palace, she stopped at a spring. Suddenly, the grief she had felt all these months overwhelmed her and she wept until she could neither move nor speak. She fell asleep by the spring.

The next morning the sound of high sweet girlish voices woke her from her sleep. Isis opened her eyes to find herself surrounded by young servant girls singing and splashing each other with water. By mistake they splashed Isis who laughed with surprise and then offered to braid their hair. As she plaited their hair, the girls almost swooned at the soft touch of her hand and the wonderful fragrance which flowed from her body.

When the servant girls returned to the palace, such a sweet scent filled the air that the queen of Byblos asked them where they had bathed. But they said that they had not bathed, they had only drawn water from the spring and an Egyptian woman had plaited their hair. The queen sent for the foreign woman and, liking her manner, made her the nurse of her youngest child. Soon the queen's older children followed Isis, for she knew songs and spells and stories; most of all, they loved her smell.

Isis came to love the queen's children and wanted to make the infant boy immortal. She nursed him with her finger. And every evening, while the others slept, she brought the infant into the hall and set him over the coals and recited a spell. As part of his body burned, she changed herself into a kite and, wailing and lamenting, flitted about the pillar which held Osiris' casket.

One night, the queen awoke, and thinking she heard the cries of her child, went into the hall. When she saw her child lying in the coals, she screamed in horror. She seized him from the fire but he was unharmed. At once, Isis resumed her womanly form and stood before the queen. "I came in search of Osiris' casket," she said. "You and your children restored me in my time of grief and I wanted to strengthen your child so he would never feel pain. But now I must return. I must bring Osiris back to his own land."

With the king's permission, the casket was removed from the pillar and given to Isis to bring back to Egypt. Isis wrapped the remains of the pillar in a linen cloth, poured ointments on it, blessed it, and gave it to the king of Byblos, who made a shrine to Isis from the pillar, which was worshiped by pilgrims for many years.

As quickly as possible, Isis had the casket placed in a boat and set sail. Maneros, the king's oldest son, who had asked to accompany Isis on her journey, sat with her by the casket as the oarsmen rowed. After a time, Isis asked him to go to the lower deck so she could be alone. When he was gone, she slowly undid the lid and opened the coffin. She looked at the body of her husband. His eyes were shut. He was wearing the green robe she had spun for him. One gold necklace encircled his chest. Isis softly touched his forehead, his eyes, his lips. She brought her face close to his and whispered:

"My brother, I am here.
My fine musician, speak to me.
Look at me.
I am your sister who loves you.
I am your sister who has been searching for you.

You are here.
To look at you is happiness.
But your face is turned away from me.
Do not separate yourself from me!
My heart is full of bitterness.

I am shouting to the heights of the heavens.
Do you not hear me?
No one on earth loved you more than I.
I was your sister, your favorite, your wife!
Speak to me, my brother, I beg you, speak!"

Maneros, hearing Isis' cries, crept quietly to the upper deck. When she felt the boy staring curiously at her ravings, she turned in great anger. The frightened boy stumbled backward, tripped, and fell over the side of the boat. The oarsmen continued to row. Isis threw herself on her husband's corpse and wept. Then she took the name-ring from Osiris' hand and closed the lid.

In Egypt, Isis hid Osiris' coffin in the swamps of the Delta in a place she thought no one would venture. But one night during the full moon, Seth was hunting in the swamps and saw what seemed to be gold glittering in the mud. He went closer, and recognizing the jeweled chest, opened it and found that the body of Osiris had been returned to Egypt and was still intact. In a fury, Seth cut the body into fourteen pieces and scattered them throughout the Delta.

When Isis heard what Seth had done, she set out with Anubis in a papyrus boat and searched the swamps until she found every part of Osiris' body, except the phallus which the sea-bream had swallowed. With her eyes closed and chanting, she used wax and spices to fashion a likeness of her husband's phallus. Then, with knotted cords, she joined his body together. She sat on Osiris and, whispering endless words of love, she revived the weariness of the listless one and drew his essence into her body. The effort was so great she fell to the earth and slept.

Then a storm poured out of the heavens. Thunder and lightning filled the air. Isis awoke, and when she realized that the gods were in terror, she ran into the storm, throwing her arms about, dancing joyously and shouting:

> "O gods! Listen to me!
> I am Isis!

I am the sister and wife of Osiris!
I wept for my husband.
I wept for my fate.
I wept for the struggle between the Two Lands.

Holy gods! I no longer weep!
I carry in my womb the seed of Osiris!
I carry in my womb the child
  who will slay his father's enemy.
He will inherit the land of Geb!
He will rule the land!
He will be your master!"

Atum, the Master of the Universe, spoke to Isis and said:
"Lady of Enchantments,
how do you know these things?
How do you know that your child
will be the god who will rule over Egypt?"

She answered:
"Am I not Isis, the most beautiful?
Am I not Isis, the mistress of charms?
Am I not the one, the only one,
who knows the secret name of Re?

My child will be blue-haired,
Great and beautiful will be his feathers.
He is already known in your hearts."

The Master of the Universe said:
"Lady of Secrets,
we do not know how you conceived.
But we acknowledge that the child

who is growing in your body belongs to Osiris.
Therefore, let no one break the egg that is growing.
Let the great magician Seth cause the child no harm."

Isis cried:

"Listen, O gods! Listen and obey the commands of Atum!
The Master of the House of Primeval Forms has spoken.
He has decreed that my son shall be protected.
He has knit together an entourage
to protect the falcon in my womb.
Atum knows that my son is the heir of Osiris.
Strength is in my flesh. Power is in my flesh.
Listen, O gods and keep him safe!"

The storm ended. Isis buried the coffin of Osiris. A short time later, Seth, who was now ruler of Upper Egypt, found Isis and brought her to the south to work in a spinning mill with other women.

After several months Thoth, the god of justice, who gives counsel, descended from the Sunboat and whispered in the ear of Isis, "Divine woman, just as mortals survive by guidance, you, too, must listen. You must not stay here any longer. Go into hiding in the northern swamps and raise your child there. When he is fully grown, let him return and take his rightful place on the throne of Osiris."

That night Isis left in the dark and made her way toward the swamps of the Delta. She walked for several weeks. Then, one evening as she was about to enter the town of Buto in the northern province, seven scorpions appeared on the road. She knew they were gods and spoke to them in a low voice, warning them, "Be careful. Do not draw attention to me. The magician Seth may be near. Do not look at anything but the road until we pass the town."

They entered Buto and passed house after house. A rich woman was standing outside her gates watching the evening light. Isis stopped, thinking to ask the woman for shelter, but when the woman saw the scorpions, she became frightened and cried, "Away, woman! Away from my door, you and your companions!" The woman shut the gates and went into her house. She gave orders to her servant not to open the doors to anyone. Isis continued. At the outskirts of Buto, a girl of the marshes saw Isis and offered her shelter.

The scorpions were angry. They spoke together and returned to the house of the rich woman. They put their poison on the spine of Tefen, the largest one. Tefen crept under the gates and double doors and entered the house of the wealthy woman.

Suddenly, there was a scream! Tefen had bitten the rich woman's son. The woman rushed out of the house with her child. She ran through the streets, calling for help. The houses remained shut. No one went to her.

Isis heard the child's cries and followed the woman. "Stop!" she cried. "I know charms. I know spells. My words have great power. My father has taught me. I can help your child. He is innocent."

The woman clutched her child to her and looked at Isis in terror. "Do not be afraid," Isis said. "Give me your child. I will heal him. Listen, and I will tell you how I learned to heal. . . .

"One day Re descended from the Sunboat and walked across the land, admiring his creations. He was old and spit dripped from his lips. I caught his spit, mixed it with mud, and fashioned a serpent. The next day when Re was walking across the earth, the serpent stung him. Re cried out in pain and fell to the ground.

" 'What is it?' the gods cried.

"For a while, the great god could not speak. His lips trembled. His body shook. He cried again, 'Help me, my children. You who were born from my body, help me! Something painful has stabbed me. My heart does not know it. My eyes have not seen it. My hands did not make it. It is not fire. It is not water. I have never tasted such pain!'

"The gods came. They brought gifts. They spoke magic words. They chanted. No one could help him.

"Then I went to him. I said, 'Tell me your name, Father, and you will be cured.'

" 'Quickly then,' he said, 'take away the poison, for I have no strength. My heart is on fire. My body is trembling. The poison spreads through me as swiftly as the Nile overflows its bank. Help me, my daughter, you are the one whose speech has the breath of life—'

" 'Tell me your secret name, Father, and you shall live.'

"Then Re spoke: 'I am abounding in names. I am abounding in forms. I am the one who made the heavens and the earth. I knotted together the mountains. I made the waters so the Heavenly Cow might come into being. I made the bull to please the cow. I stretched out the two horizons and placed the souls of the gods in the center.

" 'When I open my eyes, there is light. When I close my eyes there is darkness. The Nile rises at my command. I made the hours and days and festivals. There is no one greater than I. I am Khepri at dawn, Re at noon, Atum in the evening. These are my names.'

" 'Yes,' I said to him. 'These are your names. But tell me your secret name, the one your mother and father hid inside you when you were born so no magician might have power over you.'

"Re was silent. The hours passed. At last, in the evening when the poison ran through him like fire and he could scarcely breathe, he whispered, 'You shall have my name. Come closer so it passes from my body to yours.'

"Then he closed his eyes. There was darkness. He went

deeper and deeper into himself. He took his name from his heart and placed it in my heart. 'One day,' he said, 'you will tell my name to your son, and my name will shine in his eyes.' "

Isis then turned to the woman and said, "With Re's powers, I will cure your child."

Isis took the child from the mother's arms. Massaging his throat with salt, barley bread, and garlic, she shook him and chanted:

"Poison of Tefen, do not enter!
Poison of Befen, go into the earth!
Poison of Mesen, fall down!
Poison of Mestetef, do not penetrate!
Poison of Petet, recede!
Poison of Thetet, do not rise!
Poison of Maten, do not travel!

I am Isis, the Goddess of Magic.
All beings who sting heed my commands:
Poison, recede, withdraw——*Retreat!*"

The fire went out. The sky became clear and the poison left the child. Isis gave him back to his mother. The rich woman offered Isis gifts. Isis told her to give them to the daughter of the fisherman. The rich woman filled the hut of the marsh girl with gifts.

Six months later, in a bed of papyrus, in the presence of the sky goddesses of the Delta, Isis gave birth to Horus. She took off her red shawl and wrapped Horus in it, tying it with a magic knot to protect him. Then, she disguised herself as a beggarwoman and left Horus in the day to search for food to bring to him at night.

One evening, as Isis was returning late to Horus, she heard him crying. The *tyet* knot was undone. Saliva dripped from his mouth. Water streamed from his eyes. His body was limp. His pulse could barely be felt. Isis picked him up and put him to her breast. Her breasts were like an overflowing well, but the child could not drink.

"My child! My fatherless child! Save my child!" Isis cried. "I have left him alone too long. Surely this is the work of Seth. Who will help me?"

It was night. The gods were in the underworld. Isis cried again and let out a low moan. The fisherpeople who lived in the marshes came running from their huts. When they saw how weak the child was, they, too, wept. But no one knew how to cure him.

Then a woman who had a reputation for learning came up to Isis, carrying an ankh sign, the sign of life. "Isis, do not despair," she said. "It may not be Seth who has harmed your child. You are far in the north. In these swamps you are protected from him and his followers. Seek another cause. It may have been a scorpion or a snake that has bitten him."

Isis put her nose in Horus' mouth so she could know the smell from the inside of his body. Then she shrieked: "Poison! Horus has been poisoned!" She shook her child and leapt about the marsh like one on fire, crying to the gods:

"Re, your son has been bitten!
Your heir, the one who carries the kingship of Shu,
the infant of the marshes,
the innocent, fatherless child,
the child I watched over who gave me hope,
the child who would avenge his father's death!
Horus! Horus has been bitten!"

Isis fell to the ground. Horus cried out in pain. Everyone wept. The wailing filled the marshes. The next morning, Nephthys came running to her sister in tears.

"Isis! Isis!" she cried. "What has happened to the child? Call to the heavens! Beseech the boat of Re! Call to him and the cosmic winds will cease! Re will not sail the Sunboat while Horus is dying." Nephthys picked Isis up from the ground and said, "Speak, Mother of the God. Speak for your child!"

Then Isis let out a piercing wail. It reached the heavens. The Sunboat, the Boat of a Million Years, stopped. It did not move from its place. Thoth, the god of justice, descended and said to Isis, "Lady of Magic, you whose voice never falters, have you forgotten your power? Just because it is your own child, have you forgotten your spells? Atum has promised you. Atum has decreed that no one may harm the child."

"O Thoth," Isis said. "You have great wit, but how slowly you act. Have you brought your magic? One disaster follows another. Look how the child trembles. Seth destroyed his father. If Seth destroys the child, it will be the end of Osiris! All this time I have borne Osiris' death because I have been waiting for revenge. But now—"

"Isis, do not be afraid," Thoth said. "Nephthys, stop your wailing. I have brought the breath of life to cure the child. Keep your heart strong, child. Do not let it weaken because of the fever." Thoth then took Horus in his arms and, shaking the child, began to chant:

"The protection of Horus is the falcon who flies
in all realms.
The protection of Horus is the winged beetle in the sky.
The protection of Horus is the underworld whose faces
are reversed.
The protection of Horus is his own body.

The protection of Horus is the magic of his mother.
The protection of Horus is the names of his father.
The protection of Horus is his own name; such is the way of all sufferers.

Wake up, Horus!
The Sunboat remains in the place of yesterday.
The boat will not sail; the crew will not travel until you return to earth.
The demon of darkness will cover everything.
There will be no seasons, no shadows, no crops, no life until Horus is healed for his mother.
Poison, seep into the earth! Let all hearts rejoice!

I, Thoth, who was sent by Atum to heal Horus for his mother and for all sufferers, decree:
Poison . . . *Retreat!*
Your ka, Horus, your life force, is your protection!"

The poison left Horus. Thoth gave the child to Isis and spoke to the people, saying, "The child is cured. Go to your homes. Horus is healed to his mother's delight."

"No, wait!" Isis cried. "I beg you, Thoth, speak to the people. Ask the women who dwell in the marshes to help guard the child."

Then Thoth said, "Women who live in the province of the sky goddesses, you who loved Osiris, protect his child. Protect the child of Isis. Let no rebel harm him. Let the boy reach manhood and take his rightful place on the throne of his father.

"I must leave now for they are waiting for me on the Sunboat of Evening which will soon change to the Sunboat of Morning. I will announce to Osiris that his son is well. This news will bring joy to the gods of the Sunboat. Horus lives for his mother and for all sufferers. Horus is cured. But the fate of Horus is with you. I leave the child Horus in your protection."

At the same age Osiris had been when he set out from Egypt, Horus left the Delta for the court of Heliopolis. He stood before Re and the other gods and claimed his right to the throne of his father and to the crown of the Two Lands of Egypt.

Thoth, the god of justice, brought the double crown of Egypt to Re. Shu, the son of Re, said, "Father, Horus and Seth stand before you. Deliver your judgment. Let justice prevail over strength. Give the double-horned crown to Horus, the rightful heir."

Then Isis cried, "Oh north wind, rush to the west! Tell Osiris the news that he has been waiting to hear. Tell him his son will be king!"

"STOP!!" Re thundered. "What do you mean by deciding for yourselves? I am the Master of the Universe. The world dwells within my coils. Shu, did you not come out of my mouth? Isis, are you not the child of Geb and Nut? You are all my children. Why then do you act like this?"

The gods answered, "Horus is already wearing the name-ring of Osiris."

Seth, the son of Nut, stepped forward. He ruled Upper Egypt and he wished to rule all of Egypt. "Father," he said, "let the child prove himself. Let Horus fight with me for the throne of Egypt."

Thoth protested, "If we let them fight, and Seth is victorious, shall we give the throne to the stronger one while the rightful heir stands before us ready to be king?"

Re was silent. He preferred his lonely, brooding son, the guardian of the night. The gods sensed Re's annoyance and were silent. After a time, one of the younger gods said, "We do not know what to do. We can not take action when we do not know what is right. Let us write a letter to our mother. Let us write to Neith, the mother of Re who shone in the primeval waters. Neith is the oldest. She will know what to do."

The other gods agreed and said to the scribe Thoth, "In the name of Re, write a letter to Neith, the Oldest One."

Thoth wrote, "Atum who rules over Upper and Lower Egypt sends word to Neith, the Oldest One, the Mother of the Gods. Re wishes you to know that he passes his days attending to the business of the Two Lands and his nights worrying about Osiris. He does not see what to do. But you who shone in primeval times, you who were in the Hall of Truth when everything was decreed, tell us, what shall we do with the two who stand before us now in the tribunal? Write and give us counsel."

Neith's reply was immediate: "If you do not stop this wickedness, I will cause the sky to come crashing down on your heads. Re, double Seth's property, give your two daughters, Anath and Astarte, to Seth, and give the throne of Osiris to Horus!"

Thoth read Neith's letter to Re and the other gods. At the end of the letter, the gods cried in one voice: "The goddess is right. Neith is right. Horus shall rule over the Two Lands."

But Re, who still did not like Horus, muttered loud enough for Horus to hear, "You can hardly stand on your own feet. And your breath stinks!"

The gods were shocked at Re's insult.

Baba was the first to recover. "Re," he said, "have you looked at your own shrine lately? It's empty! No one goes there anymore."

Re was hurt. He left the hall and went to his tent and sulked.

The gods turned on Baba, the Ram God, and said, "Go away! You have committed a serious offense disturbing Re."

The gods went to their tents and slept.

Re laid on his back and brooded.

Then the great goddess Hathor, the Lady of Love, poked her head into Re's tent and winked. She smiled mischievously. She tiptoed into the tent, and grinning, lifted up her skirt, revealing her private parts. "Lookie, Lookie!" she squealed. "Look and see!" Still giggling, she skipped out of the tent. Re could not keep from laughing. His laugh rose up in his belly and bounced about the tent until he stood up.

Re went back to the assembly and said to Seth and Horus, "Speak and we will listen to you."

Seth, son of Nut, came forward. "I am the strongest of the gods. Every day, at dawn and sunset, I stand at the helm of the Sunboat and with my spear I ward off the attacks of Apopis, the serpent of darkness. If it were not for me, Apopis would devour the Sunboat. No other god dares do what I do."

The gods all said, "That is true. Seth is right!"

Baba, the Ram God, said, "Shall we give the throne of Egypt to a boy, while his older relative, a man who can rule, is here?"

Thoth said, "Shall we give the throne to the uncle while the son is alive?"

"This is not fair," falcon-faced Horus protested. "You are mistreating me and cheating me of my father's throne."

Then Isis began to swear, "By my mother Neith, I shall take this matter to the Sunboat. I will go to Atum, in his form of Khepri, the Becoming One, and he will see that justice prevails. My husband has been murdered! Have you all forgotten who united the Two Lands? Have you forgotten who brought order and abundance to Egypt? Who gave you food to eat and beer to drink? Osiris taught the people to serve and honor you. And now you refuse to honor his son. When will justice be heard?"

"Isis! Isis!" the gods tried to quiet her. "Be calm, the one who is right will be given his due."

Then Seth shouted, "If this woman is not forced to leave the court, I will take my spear weighing four thousand and five hundred pounds and ram it through one of you every day!"

Re said, "The assembly is over. Go to the Island-in-the-Midst and decide among yourselves. And tell the ferryman not to transport any woman across the water who looks in any way like Isis."

The gods crossed over to the Island-in-the-Midst and began to eat bread.

Isis went to the ferryman. She had changed herself into a bent old woman. She wore a gold ring on her hand. She spoke in a low, cracked voice, "I am bringing a jar of barley to my young son who has been looking after cattle on the island for the past five days. He is very hungry."

The ferryman said, "I have been told to ferry no woman across the water."

"Were you not told to ferry no woman who looks like Isis?"

"All women resemble Isis. What will you give me if I take you across the water?"

"I will give you a loaf of bread."

"Hah! A loaf of bread! What is a loaf of bread to me when I have been told to ferry no woman across the water and you are wearing a gold ring?"

"Then I will give you the gold ring."

The ferryman took the ring and rowed her across to the Island-in-the-Midst. Isis tripped across the sands to the trees. Through the trees she saw the gods sitting and feasting in the arbor of the Master of the Universe. Then, with her magic, she transformed herself into a young woman with a slender inviting figure, a woman so beguiling, so tempting, that no one who saw her could resist her. She stepped out from behind the trees. Seth was the only one who saw her. His eyes opened. His loins stirred.

Quickly, Seth got up and went toward her. He hid behind a

tree near her and whispered, "Young woman, come closer. I want to speak to you. Wait! Stop! Do not flee! You are as beautiful as a goddess. You . . . I . . . wait! Tell me your name!"

Then Isis stopped flitting from tree to tree and walked demurely toward him. She tilted her head and spoke shyly, "Kind lord, please help me. I am a poor widow. I was married to a cowherd and bore him a son. When the boy's father died, the child looked after his father's cattle. Then a stranger came and stayed with me. But now this stranger has told my son, 'I want your father's cattle and I will take them. As for you, I will beat you and chase you away!' Oh kind lord, I hope you will be my son's champion. What can I do to persuade you?"

"This is not just!" Seth cried indignantly. "No stranger should inherit a man's cattle while the son is alive. I will strike the stranger in the face and give the cattle to your son!"

"YAAA-AAAH!!!" Isis let out a shriek. She threw up her arms and, transforming herself into a kite, perched in the branches of an acacia tree, shouting, "It is done! Justice has been spoken! Seth, you have judged yourself. You have judged yourself! Weep now for the cleverness of your own words."

Seth burst into tears. Whimpering, he returned to Re.

"What is it now?" Re asked.

"Father, she has done it again. She has tricked me. She changed herself into a shy, beautiful woman. Who could resist her? She said to me, 'I am a poor widow. My husband died and my son was taking care of the cattle, but then a stranger came and wanted to keep the cattle for himself and to throw out my son.' That is what she said."

"And what did you reply?" Re asked.

"Yes, what did I say? I said, 'It is not right to give the cattle to a stranger when the son of the father is still alive!' I said, 'I would strike the stranger in the face and set the son in the father's place!' "

"Oh my son, you have judged yourself," Re said. "Since you have judged yourself, what can I do for you?"

"Punish the ferryman! Bring him to court and let him be asked, 'Why did you ferry that woman across the water?' "

So the ferryman was brought to court and tried. His toes were cut off as a punishment for his greed, and gold became an abomination to him forever.

The gods crossed over to the other side of the river and journeyed south along the Nile. They sat near a mountain by the shore and watched the hippopotamuses. They watched them sink under the water. They watched the bubbles rise to the top. And they took bets as to which hippopotamus would stay down the longest.

Then Re sent them a message. He said, "*What* are you doing? These two will spend the rest of their lives wrangling while you watch the bubbles rise and fall. Seth has already judged himself. When my letter reaches you, give the double crown of Egypt to Horus."

The gods said, "Re is right. Re has given his decree. Horus shall be given the throne of Osiris." The gods were about to place the crown on Horus' head when Seth shouted, "No! Not while I am alive! Not while the defender of the kingdom is alive will you place the crown on the child's head. Look at the mama's boy! Why, he never leaves his mother's side. Upstart! Brat! Are you afraid to be tested? Let us change ourselves into hippopotamuses, and the one who stays down under the water three months shall be king."

"I am not afraid!" Horus cried.

Then the two changed themselves into hippopotamuses and dove into the water.

Isis shouted, "He will kill my son. Seth will kill my son!" She ran about on the shore weeping, but since the others ignored her, she took action. She braided hemp into a rope, pounded metal to make a harpoon's head and attached the rope to the harpoon. Then she threw the cable into the water.

The barb struck Horus.

"Mother!!" Horus shouted. "It's me! You have hit me! Release the barb. It's your son Horus."

"Barb!" Isis said. "Release him. It is my son Horus."

The barb rose from the water and Isis cast it again.

The barb pierced the body of Seth.

"What have you done?" Seth cried out. "Sister, order your barb to release me. I am not a stranger. I am your brother, we have the same mother. Our mother cared for me as she cared for you."

Isis was jolted. Seth was her enemy. But Seth was also the son of her mother. As she had loved and cared for Horus, so had Nut loved and cared for Seth.

Seth called to her again, "Isis! Release the barb! Release the barb! I am the son of your mother. I am your brother."

Isis said, "Barb, release him. He is my brother Seth."

Then Horus rose from the water full of rage. His face was as savage as a panther from Upper Egypt. He went onto the shore and took an axe, a great axe. He swung the axe and cut off the head of his mother. Then he rushed up the side of the mountain, weeping.

The gods watched in astonishment.

Re said, "Who is that woman?"

Isis had changed herself into a statue of flint without a head.

"My lord Re," Thoth said, "it is the mighty Isis. In his anger, Horus cut off her head." Then Thoth placed a helmet in the shape of a cow's head on Isis' shoulders and the horns became her crown.

Re said, "Find Horus and punish him for this horrendous deed."

The gods climbed the mountain looking for Horus. Seth

found Horus hiding under a *shenusha* tree in an oasis. He threw Horus to the ground and tore out his eyes. In the night, Horus' two eyes shone up at Seth. Seth buried them in the earth. Then he went down the mountain. When the gods questioned him, he lied and said, "I could not find him." At dawn, in the place where Seth had buried Horus' eyes, two white lilies grew.

Horus did not return. The gods were uneasy. Then the goddess Hathor went up the mountain to look for Horus. She found him lying near the *shenusha* tree, gasping in pain. She went into the desert. She caught a gazelle, an animal of Seth, and milked it. Then she said to Horus, "Open your eyes and I will put in these drops." She put two drops of gazelle's milk in his right eye and two drops in his left eye. Then she said to Horus, "Close your eyes." Horus closed his eyes. When he opened them again, he could see.

Hathor returned to the gods and said, "I found Horus. Seth had torn out his eyes and he was in great pain, but I have restored his sight." The gods waited.

After a time, Horus returned and the gods said, "Let us go back to Heliopolis."

In the court, Re spoke to Horus and Seth and said, "Enough. Stop your fighting. Eat. Drink. Spend your days in peace."

"Yes," Seth agreed. "It is enough. Come, brother, I will make a banquet for you at my house. Spend a happy day with me."

"Yes," Horus said. "It is time to do so."

Seth and Horus feasted all day. That night a bed was spread for them and they lay down together. In the night, Seth stroked his phallus and it became stiff. He placed his phallus between the loins of Horus. But Horus was awake and put his hands between his legs and caught Seth's semen.

In the morning, Horus went to his mother who was walking

by the Nile. Isis' head had been restored, but she still wore cow's horns as a crown. Horus said to her, "Mother, look what Seth has done to me." He opened his hand and showed her Seth's semen.

Isis cried out in horror. She seized her knife and cut off Horus' hand and threw it into the water. Then she drew out another hand for Horus and spread some sweet ointment on Horus' penis. The penis became stiff. She put a jar over it and caught Horus' semen. She took the semen to Seth's house and asked the gardener, "Which is Seth's favorite plant?"

"Lettuce," the gardener said. "Seth prefers lettuce."

So Isis spread Horus' semen on the lettuces.

Later that afternoon, Seth came home and ate lettuce and became pregnant with Horus' semen.

The next day Seth said to Horus, "Let us go to court, for there is more to be said."

"Willingly," Horus agreed.

They went to court and Re said, "Speak, both of you."

Seth began, "Let the throne of Egypt be given to me, for the other man standing before you is not a man. She is a woman. Last night Horus played the slave girl as I performed the work of a man."

When they heard this, the gods laughed and belched and spat at Horus, but Horus also laughed. Then he said, "Yes, yes, it is true. One man is standing before you and also one woman. But look again for the woman. The woman Seth is lying. Summon our seed and you will see who is the man and who is the woman."

Thoth, the god of justice, put his hand on Horus' arm and said, "Seed of Seth, come forth."

"Here," a faint voice spoke.

"Where?" asked the gods, turning around.

"Here," the faint voice spoke again.

The gods began to search the assembly hall.

"Here," the voice said. "Here."

The gods wandered out of the court toward the river.

"Here I am." The voice was louder.

They found the seed of Seth in the water and they laughed. Then they returned to court.

Thoth put his hand on Seth's arm and said, "Seed of Horus, come forth."

The seed of Horus said, "Where shall I give birth?"

"On Seth's ear," one of the gods said.

The seed objected. "That is not a proper place for a divine seed."

"Then from his forehead," Thoth said.

But the seed of Horus had a mind of its own and emerged as a beautiful light on the top of Seth's head. Seth was angry and tried to brush it off. Thoth took the golden light and put it on his own head and it became his crown.

The gods then called out, "Horus is right. Seth is wrong!" But before they could give the crown to Horus, Seth cried, "The court shall not give the crown to Horus until he has fought with me."

"Willingly!" Horus said.

Seth said, "We will make stone ships and race them. Whoever wins, shall be king."

Horus secretly made a cedar ship which he covered with gypsum. At sunset, he set it by the shore. The next morning when Seth saw Horus' ship he thought it was stone. So he climbed a great mountain and cut off its peak. From the peak, he carved a gigantic stone ship.

The gods assembled. The ships were pushed out into the water. Seth's ship sank immediately. Horus' ship floated. Seth disappeared. Then a hippopotamus rose from the water and turned Horus' ship over. Horus took a barb and threw it at the hippopotamus. "No, Horus," the gods cried. "You are right. But do not kill Seth."

Horus shouted, "What kind of court is this? For eighty years I have been fighting for my father's throne. For eighty years my mother has waited for my father to be avenged. For eighty years, I have been told, 'Horus is right. Seth is wrong!' And still, I have not been given the throne! I will not wait for justice from this court. I will go to the divine mother, Neith."

Thoth said, "This can go on no longer. Egypt has been without a king for eighty years. Strife and disorder rule the Two Lands. Re, send a letter to Osiris. Let him judge between them."

"Write to Osiris," Re commanded Thoth.

When the letter was read to Osiris in the underworld, he gave a great shout. He replied at once, "Re, why do you mistreat my son? I am the one who made you strong. I am the one who nourished you and your gods with barley and emmer."

Re told Thoth to reply with these words, "Osiris, if you had never come into existence, if you had never been born, barley and emmer would still exist."

Osiris answered, "Re, what you have created is good. But as for justice, it has disappeared from the earth. Yet, where I live there are savage-faced messengers who fear neither god nor goddess. If I send them, they will bring me the heart of anyone who does wrong. Re, when you created the stars, did you not tell them that they would find their resting place with me? When you created the gods, did you not tell them that they would find their final resting place with me? Since all of you must come before me, why do you act as if your deeds will not be weighed?"

When the gods heard this, they said, "Osiris is right! Horus is right! Seth is wrong!"

But Seth said in a low voice, "Let Horus fight with me on the Island-in-the-Midst."

They went to the Island-in-the-Midst. They wrestled. At first

Seth pinned Horus, but Horus slipped out of Seth's grasp. Then Horus pinned Seth. After all these years, Seth was not as agile or quick as he had been and Horus held Seth fast. Seth could not defeat Horus.

Re then summoned Isis to Heliopolis and said, "Bring Seth to me bound in ropes." Isis removed her cow's horns and chose to wear a golden crown. For the first time in many years, she dressed herself in fine linen clothes and jewelry. She led her husband's enemy bound like a prisoner to the court of Re.

Re spoke to Seth and said, "Why do you insist on force? Why do you refuse the judgment you yourself made?"

"Father, I accept the judgment. Let the throne of Osiris be given to Horus, the son of Isis."

Horus was brought to court. Thoth placed the double crown, the crown of Upper and Lower Egypt, on Horus' head. Horus mounted the steps and sat on the throne of his father. The gods knelt before him and said, "You will be king of the Two Lands. You will be king forever, to the end."

Isis' heart was swelling with joy. She said to Horus, "Osiris is at peace. The gods will serve you. Govern the people wisely. Nourish the people and be guided by the holy Eye of the Lady of the Crown."

Thoth said, "Horus has been given the throne. What shall be given to Seth?"

Re said, "Seth, the son of Nut, will be my son. He will stay with me. He will be the thunder that roars in the sky and all the people will fear him."

"Rejoice! Rejoice!" the gods cried. "Rejoice throughout the land before Horus, the son of Isis!" The gods placed garlands of flowers around Horus' neck. Falcon-faced Horus was strewn with lotus blossoms and melilote flowers.

Isis cried, "Horus is king. Heaven is filled with joy. The earth rejoices. Horus has been given the throne of his father. Osiris, my husband, Horus is king!"

Then Horus, the King of Egypt, sent a message to his father in the underworld:

"My father, the gates of the sky are open.
The gates of the sky are flung wide open.
Listen to what I have done for you:

I have struck the one who struck you.
I have bound the one who bound you.
Seth will now serve you.
Seth's breeze will carry your boat across the water.
Sorrow is at an end in the Two Lands.
Rise, my father!

The gods are dancing for you,
They strike their flesh,
They clap their hands,
They loosen their hair,
They crouch,
They leap,
They say:

'Rise, Osiris!
You went away, but now you have returned.
Rise, Osiris!
You were asleep, but now you are awake.
Rise, Osiris!
You died, but now you live again.'

You rise from the earth—the plant of life.
You strengthen the people.
You sustain the living.

The love of you is in the fields,
in the water, in the sky.

Isis did not forget you.
She searched the earth until she found you.
She gathered together your flesh.
She rejoices for the life which rises once again from you.
Isis is now content.
Sorrow is at an end in the Two Lands.
Rise, my father!"

Osiris then took his place on the Sunboat.

Isis and Horus went to the temple of Heliopolis which had been built on the First Hill. Horus lifted up the fallen *djed* pillar of Osiris, and it stood erect. Isis wrapped her red shawl in a *tyet* knot around the pillar. She blessed Horus, and as she did so, she placed Re's secret name in his heart.

INANNA AND DUMUZI

The Sacred Marriage Rite

For Rachel Cloudstone Zucker

In the first days,
In the first nights,
In the first years,
When everything needed was brought into being,
When everything needed was properly nourished,
When heaven moved away from earth,
When earth separated from heaven,
And the name of man was fixed—
When the Sky God, An, carried off the heavens,
When the Air God, Enlil, carried off the earth,
And the Queen of the Great Below, Ereshkigal, was given
the underworld for her domain,
Then Enki, the God of Wisdom, set sail for the underworld.
Windstones were tossed against him,
Hailstorms were hurled up against him,
The waters of the sea struck his boat like lions. . . .

At that time, a tree, a single tree, a *huluppu*-tree
Was planted by the banks of the Euphrates.
The waters of the Euphrates nourished the tree.
The whirling South Wind arose;

Pulling at the roots and ripping at the branches
Until the waters of the Euphrates carried it away.

A young woman walking by the banks of the river
Plucked the tree from the water and said:
"I will take this tree to my city, Uruk
I will plant this tree in my holy garden."

The young woman, Inanna, planted the tree.
She cared for the tree with her hand.
She settled the earth around the tree with her foot.
She wondered:
"How long will it be until I have a shining throne
to sit upon?
How long will it be until I have a shining bed
to lie upon?"

Five years passed, ten years.
The tree grew thick,
But its bark did not split.

Then a serpent who could not be charmed
Made his nest in the roots of the tree.
The *Anzu* bird set his young in the branches.
And the dark woman, Lilith, built her home in the trunk.

The young woman who loved to laugh wept.
All night Inanna wept.
But the creatures would not leave her tree.

As the birds began to sing at the coming of dawn,
The Sun God, Utu, started across the heavens.
Inanna called to her brother, Utu, for help.
Utu, the valiant warrior, would not help his sister.

As the birds began to sing at the coming of the second dawn,
Gilgamesh, the valiant warrior, walked across the land.
Inanna called to Gilgamesh for help.
Gilgamesh, the hero of Uruk, stood by Inanna.

He fastened his armor weighing sixty pounds around his chest;
The sixty pounds were as little to him as sixty feathers.
He lifted his "bronze axe" of the road to his shoulder;
The bronze axe weighed three hundred and fifty pounds.
He entered Inanna's holy garden.

Gilgamesh struck the serpent who could not be charmed.
The *Anzu* bird flew with his young to the mountains;
Lilith smashed her home and fled to the wild, uninhabited places.
Then Gilgamesh loosened the roots of the *huluppu*-tree,
The sons of the city, who accompanied him, cut off the branches.

From the trunk of the tree he carved for her a throne,
From the trunk of the tree Gilgamesh carved for Inanna a bed.
And she, from the roots of the tree, fashioned for him a drum,
And from the branches she fashioned a drumstick.
Inanna gave Gilgamesh the drum and drumstick.
The mighty warrior gave the young woman a shining throne.
Gilgamesh gave to Inanna a shining bed.

The brother spoke to his younger sister.
Utu, the Sun God, spoke to Inanna and said:
"Young Lady, the flax in its fullness is lovely,
Inanna, the grain is glistening in its furrow.
I will hoe it for you. I will bring it to you;
A piece of linen is always needed."

"Brother, if you bring me the flax,
Who will spin it for me?"

"Sister, I will bring it to you spun."

"Brother, if you bring it to me spun,
Who will braid it for me?"

"Sister, I will bring it to you braided."

"Utu, if you bring it to me braided,
Who will weave it for me?"

"Inanna, I will bring it to you woven."

"Brother, if you bring it to me woven,
Who will bleach it for me?"

"Sister, I will bring it to you bleached."

"Brother, if you bring me my bridal sheet,
Who will go to bed with me?
Utu, who will go to bed with me?"

"Your bridegroom will go to bed with you!
He who was conceived on the sacred marriage throne,
Dumuzi, the shepherd! He will go to bed with you!"

Inanna spoke:
"No, brother!
The man of my heart is the farmer."

Utu spoke:
"Sister, marry the shepherd! Why are you unwilling?
His cream is good; his milk is good.
Whatever he touches shines brightly.
Inanna, marry the shepherd."

Inanna answered:
"I will not marry the shepherd!
His clothes are coarse. His wool is rough.
I will marry the farmer.
The farmer grows flax for my clothes,
The farmer grows barley for my table.
I will marry the farmer!"

Then, Dumuzi appeared and said:
"What is all this talk about the farmer?
If he gives you flour,
I will give you wool.
If he gives you beer,
I will give you sweet milk.
If he gives you bread,
I will give you honey cheese."

Inanna said:
"Shepherd, without my mother, Ningal,
you'd be driven away
Without my father, Nanna,
you'd have no roof over your head
Without my brother, Utu—"

Dumuzi spoke:
"Inanna, do not start a quarrel.
My father, Enki, is as good as your father,
My mother, Sirtur, is as good as your mother,
My sister, Geshtinanna, is as good as yours.
I am as good as your brother, Utu.
Queen of the palace, let us talk it over."

The word they had spoken
Was a word of desire.
From the starting of the quarrel
Came the lovers' desire.

The shepherd brought cream to the royal house,
Dumuzi brought milk to the royal house.
He stood outside the door. He called:
"Open the house, my lady. Open the house!"

Inanna ran to her mother who bore her. She said:
"What shall I do?"

Ningal counseled her, saying:
"My child, the young man will treat you like a father.
He will care for you like a mother.
Open the house, my lady. Open the house!"

At her mother's command,
Inanna bathed and anointed herself with scented oil.
She put on her royal white robe.
She arranged her lapis beads around her neck.

She prepared her dowry.
She took her seal in her hand.

Dumuzi waited expectantly.

Inanna opened the door for him.
Inside the house she shone before him
Like the light of the moon.

Dumuzi gazed at her joyously,
He pressed his neck close against hers,
He kissed her.

Inanna sang:

"What I tell you
Let the singer weave into song.
Let it pass from old to young
Let it flow from ear to mouth
Let my bridegroom rejoice:

My vulva, the horn,
The Boat of Heaven
Is full of eagerness like the young moon.
My untilled land lies fallow.

As for me, the young woman,
Who will plow my vulva?
Who will plow my high field?
Who will plow my wet ground?

As for me, Inanna,
Who will plow my vulva?
Who will station the ox there?
Who will plow my vulva?"

Dumuzi:

"Great Lady, the king will plow your vulva!
I, Dumuzi, the king, will plow your vulva!"

Inanna:

"Then plow my vulva, man of my heart!
Plow my vulva!"

In the king's lap, the rising cedar stood.
Plants grew high by their side,
Grains grew high by their side,
Gardens flourished luxuriantly.

Inanna sang:

"He has sprouted; he has burgeoned;
He is lettuce planted by the water,
He is the one my womb loves best.

My well-stocked garden of the plain,
My barley growing high in its furrow,
My apple tree bearing fruit to its crown,
He is the one my womb loves best.

My honeyman, my honeyman sweetens me always,
My honeyman is the lord of the gods.
His hand is honey; his foot is honey,
He is the one my womb loves best."

Dumuzi sang:

"O Lady, your breast is your field,
Inanna, your breast is your field,
Your broad field pours out plants,
Your broad field pours out grain.

Water flows from on high for your servant,
Bread flows from on high for your servant,
Pour it out for me, Inanna,
I will drink all you offer."

Inanna:

"Make your milk sweet and thick, my bridegroom,
My shepherd, I will drink your fresh milk.
Let your goat's milk flow in my sheepfold.
Fill my holy churn with your honey cheese.
Wild bull Dumuzi, I will drink your fresh milk.

My husband, I will guard my sheepfold for you.
I will watch over your house of life, the storehouse,
The shining quivering place which delights Sumer,
The house which decides the fates of the land,
The house which gives the breath of life to the people.
I, the queen of the palace, will watch
over your house."

Dumuzi:

"My sister, I will take you to my garden,
Inanna, I will take you to my garden.
I will take you to my orchard,
I will take you to my apple tree,
There I will plant the sweet, honey-covered seed."

Inanna:

"My brother brought me into his garden,
Dumuzi brought me into his garden.
I strolled with him among the standing trees,
I stood with him by the fallen trees,
By an apple tree I knelt as is proper.

Before my brother coming in song
Who came to me out of the poplar leaves
Who rose to me in the midday heat
Before my lord Dumuzi,
    I poured out plants from my womb.
I placed grain before him!
I placed plants before him!
I poured out grain before him!
I poured out plants before him!
I poured out plants from my womb!"

Inanna sang:

"Last night as I the queen was shining bright,
As I was shining bright and dancing,
Singing praises at the coming of the night—
My lord Dumuzi met me.
He placed his hand in mine,
He pressed his neck close to mine.

My high priest, you are ready for the holy loins.
The plants and herbs in your field are ripe.
O Dumuzi! Your fullness is my delight!"

She called for it, she called for it, she called for the bed!
She called for the bed that rejoices the heart!
She called for the bed that sweetens the loins!
She called for the bed of kingship!
She called for the bed of queenship!

Inanna spread the bridal sheet across the royal bed.
She said:

"My king, the bed is ready."

She said:
"My bridegroom, the bed is waiting!"

He put his hand to her hand.
He put his hand to her heart.
Sweet is the sleep of hand to hand.
Sweeter still the sleep of heart to heart.

She bathed for the wild bull,
She bathed for the shepherd Dumuzi,
She perfumed her skin with ointment,
She coated her mouth with sweet-smelling amber,
She painted her eyes with kohl.

He shaped her loins with his soft hands,
The shepherd Dumuzi filled her lap with cream
and milk,
He stroked her pubic hair,
He watered her womb.

With his hands, he held her full vulva,
He smoothed her black boat with cream,
He quickened her narrow boat with milk,
He caressed Inanna on the bed.

Then she caressed the high priest on the bed,
Inanna caressed the faithful shepherd Dumuzi,
She caressed his loins, the shepherdship of the land,
She decreed a sweet fate for him.

Inanna, The First Daughter of The Moon,
The heroic woman, greater than her mother,
Inanna, who was presented the *me* by the God of Wisdom,

Inanna, the Queen of Heaven, decreed the fate of Dumuzi:
"In battle, I am your leader
In combat, I am your armor-bearer
In the assembly, I am your advocate
On the campaign, I am your inspiration.
In all ways you are fit:

To sit on the lapis throne
To wear the crown on your head
To race on the road with the holy scepter in your hand
To wear the holy sandals on your feet
To prance on the holy breast like a lapis calf.

May what An has determined for you not be altered
May what Enlil has granted for you not be changed
You are the choice of Ningal
You are the choice of my heart."

Ninshubur, the faithful servant of Inanna,
Led Dumuzi to the sweet thighs of Inanna.
She said:
"My queen, here is your beloved bridegroom,
May he spend long days in the sweetness
of your holy loins.
Grant him a favorable and glorious reign
Give him the king's throne, which is firm
in its foundations
Grant him the shepherd's staff of judgment
Grant him the enduring crown with the radiant diadem.

From where the sun rises to where the sun sets
From the south to the north
From the land of the *huluppu* to the land of the cedar
Let his shepherd's staff protect all of Sumer and Akkad.

In the marshland let the fish and birds chatter
In the canebrake let the old and young reeds grow high
In the steppe let the trees grow high
In the forests let the deer and wild goats multiply
In the orchards let there be wine and honey
In the gardens let the lettuce and cress grow high
In the palace let there be long life
In the canals let the Tigris and Euphrates flow
Let the plants grow high and fill the meadows
Let the Lady of Vegetation pile the grain high.

With lifted head, he went to the holy loins,
With lifted head, the king went to the holy loins of Inanna.
After he had pleased her,
Dumuzi held Inanna, the Holy Priestess of Heaven, in his arms.

Inanna spoke:
"My beloved, the delight of my eyes, you met me.
We rejoiced together.
You took your pleasure of me.

You brought me into your house,
You laid me down on your fragrant honey-bed.
Lying by my heart, tongue-playing,
One by one, fifty times you did so.

Now, my sweet love is sated.
Now you say:
'Set me free, my sister,
You will be a little daughter to my father.
My beloved sister, I must go to the palace.
Set me free, Inanna, set me free.'

My blossom-bearer, your allure was sweet,
My blossom-bearer in the apple orchard,
My bearer of fruit in the apple orchard,
Dumuzi-*abzu,* your allure was sweet.

My fearless one,
My shining one,
How sweet was your allure . . ."

From the Great Above, she opened her ear to the Great Below.
From the Great Above, the goddess opened her ear to
the Great Below.
From the Great Above, Inanna opened her ear to
the Great Below.
She abandoned heaven and earth to descend to the underworld.
The Holy Priestess of Heaven abandoned her seven temples
and her seven cities.
Inanna gathered together the *me*.
She advised her trusted servant:
"Ninshubur, I am descending now to the underworld.
If I do not return,
Go to Father Enlil, the Air God.
If he will not help,
Go to Father Nanna, the Moon God.
If he will not help,
Go to Father Enki. Father Enki is the God of Wisdom.
He knows the food of life. He knows the water of life.
Surely he will not let me die.
Ninshubur, heed my words."

When Inanna arrived at the outer gates of the underworld,
She knocked loudly.
She cried in a fierce voice:
"Open the door, gatekeeper!
Open the door, Neti!
I alone would enter!"

Neti entered the palace of Ereshkigal. He said:
"My queen, a young woman,
As tall as heaven,
As wide as the earth,
As strong as the foundations of the city walls,
Waits outside the palace gates.

She carries the *me.*
She says she has come to witness the funeral rites."

When Ereshkigal, the Queen of the Underworld, heard this,
She slapped her thigh and bit her lip.
She took the matter into her heart and dwelt on it.
Then she spoke:
"Neti, my chief gatekeeper of the underworld,
Bolt the seven gates of the underworld.
Then, one by one, open each gate a crack.
Let Inanna enter;
As she enters, remove her royal garments.
Let the Holy Priestess of Heaven enter bowed low."

Neti opened the outer gate and said:
"Come, Inanna, enter."

When Inanna entered the first gate,
The crown of the steppe was removed from her head.
Inanna asked:
"What is this?"

She was told:
"Quiet, Inanna, the ways of the underworld are perfect.
They may not be questioned."

When Inanna entered the second gate,
Her lapis beads were removed from her neck.

When she entered the third gate,
Her double strand of beads was removed from her breast.

When she entered the fourth gate,
Her breastplate, called "Come, man, come!" was removed from her chest.

When she entered the fifth gate,
Her gold ring was removed from her wrist.

When she entered the sixth gate,
Her lapis measuring rod and line was removed from her hand.
At each gate, Inanna asked:
"What is this?"

At each gate, she was told:
"Quiet, Inanna, the ways of the underworld are perfect.
They may not be questioned."

When Inanna entered the seventh gate,
Her royal white robe was removed from her body.

Naked and bowed low, Inanna entered the throne room.
Ereshkigal rose from her throne.
As Inanna started toward the throne,
The judges of the underworld surrounded her;
Passing judgment against her.

Then Ereshkigal fastened on Inanna the eye of death.
She spoke against her the word of wrath.
She uttered against her the cry of guilt.

She struck her.

Inanna was turned into a corpse,
A piece of rotting meat,
And was hung from a hook on the wall.

After three days and three nights when Inanna did not return,
Ninshubur set up a lament by the ruins.
She beat the drum in the assembly places.
She dressed herself in a single garment like a beggar.
Alone, she went to Nippur and the temple of Enlil.
When she entered the holy shrine,
She pleaded:
"O Father Enlil, do not let your bright silver
be covered with the dust of the underworld.
Do not let the Holy Priestess of Heaven be put to death
in the underworld."

Father Enlil answered:
"My daughter craved the Great Above.
Inanna craved the Great Below.
She who goes to the Dark City does not return."
Father Enlil would not help.

Ninshubur went to Ur and the temple of Nanna.
When Inanna entered the holy shrine,
She pleaded:
"O Father Nanna, do not let your precious lapis
be broken into stone for the stoneworker.
Do not let the Holy Priestess of Heaven be put to death
in the underworld."

Father Nanna said:
"My daughter craved the Great Above.
Inanna craved the Great Below.
She who receives the *me* of the underworld does not
return."
Father Nanna would not help.

Ninshubur went to Eridu and the temple of Enki.
When she entered the holy shrine,
She pleaded:
"O Father Enki, do not let your fragrant boxwood
be cut into wood for the woodworker.
Do not let the Holy Priestess of Heaven be put to death
in the underworld."

Father Enki said:
"Inanna? The Holy Priestess of Heaven?
What has my daughter done? What has happened?
I am troubled. I am grieved."

From under his fingernail, Father Enki brought forth dirt.
He fashioned the dirt into a *kurgarra,*
  a creature neither male nor female,
From under the fingernail of his other hand,
  he brought forth dirt.
He fashioned a *galatur,*
  a creature neither male nor female.

Like flies, the two creatures slipped
Through the cracks of the underworld.
They entered the throne room of Ereshkigal.

Her breasts were bare.
No linen covered her body.
Her hair swirled around her head like leeks.

Ereshkigal, the Queen of the Underworld, was moaning
With the cries of a woman about to give birth:
  "Oh! Oh, my inside!"

The creatures moaned, too:
  "Oh! Oh, your inside!"

She groaned:
  "Ohh! Ohhh! My outside!"

They groaned, too:
  "Ohh! Ohhh! Your outside!"

She sighed:
  "Ah! Ah! My heart!"

They sighed, too:
"Ah! Ah! Your heart!"

She panted:
"Ahh-hh! Ahh! My liver!"

They panted:
"Ahh-hh! Ahh! Your liver!"

She stopped.
She looked at him, she said:
"Who are you, moaning and groaning with me?
I like you.
I will give you a gift.
I will give you the grain gift, the fields in harvest."
I will give you the water gift, the river in its fullness."

The *kugarra* and the *galatur* answered:
"We do not want it."

She said:
"Speak then. What do you want?"

They answered:
"We want only the corpse
That hangs from the hook on the wall."

She said:
"The corpse belongs to Inanna."

They answered:
"Whether it belongs to our queen,
Whether it belongs to our king,
That is what we wish."

The corpse was given to them.

The *kurgarra* sprinkled the food of life on the corpse.
The *galatur* sprinkled the water of life on the corpse.
Inanna arose.

Inanna was about to ascend,
When the judges of the underworld seized her. They said:
"No one returns from the underworld unmarked.
If Inanna would return, she must provide someone in
her place."

As Inanna ascended from the underworld,
The *galla* clung to her side.
The *galla* are demons who know no food, who know no drink,
Who eat no offerings, who drink no libations,
Who accept no gifts.
They enjoy no lovemaking,
They have no sweet children to kiss,
They tear the wife from the husband's arms,
They tear the child from the father's knee,
They steal the bride from her marriage home,
They followed Inanna. They clung to her side.

At the outer gates of the underworld,
Ninshubur, dressed in a soiled sackcloth,
waited for Inanna.

The *galla* said:
"Walk on, Inanna. We will take Ninshubur
in your place."

Inanna refused:
"No! Not Ninshubur! Because of her my life was saved.
She heeded my words. I will never give her to you."

At the holy shrine of Badtibira,
Lulal, the son of Inanna, dressed in a soiled sackcloth,
Was mourning for his mother.

The *galla* said:
"Walk on Inanna. We will take Lulal in your place."

Inanna refused:
"No! Not Lulal! He is a leader among men.
He is my right hand. He is my left hand.
I will never give him to you."

At the big apple tree in Uruk,
Dumuzi was dressed in shining garments.
He was seated on his royal throne.
When he saw Inanna, he did not move.

The *galla* seized him by the thighs.
They poured milk from his churn.
They broke the reed pipe the shepherd was playing.

Then, Inanna fastened on Dumuzi the eye of death.
She spoke against him the word of wrath.
She uttered against him the cry of guilt:
"Take Dumuzi! Take him away!"

The *galla* seized Dumuzi.
They made him stand up. They made him sit down.
They beat the husband of Inanna.
They gashed him with axes.

Dumuzi cried out to Utu, the Sun God:
"Utu, you are a just god,
I am the husband of your sister!
I brought milk to Ningal's house,
I brought food to the holy shrine,
I danced on the holy knees, the knees of Inanna.
Change my hands to snake hands,
Change my feet to snake feet,
Do not let them hold me."

The merciful Utu accepted Dumuzi's tears.
He changed Dumuzi's hands to snake hands.
He changed Dumuzi's feet to snake feet.
Dumuzi escaped.

His heart was filled with tears,
The shepherd's heart was filled with tears,
Dumuzi's heart was filled with tears.

He stumbled across the steppe, weeping:
"O steppe, set up a wail for me,
Crabs in the river, mourn for me,
Frogs in the river, call for me,
O, my mother, Sirtur, weep for me.
If my mother does not know the day I am dead,
You, O steppe, tell her—tell my mother."

He lay down to rest,
The shepherd lay down to rest.
Among the buds and bushes, he fell asleep.

He dreamed a dream.
He awoke from his dream, terrified.

He called for his sister, Geshtinanna,
The singer who knows many songs,
The scribe who knows the meaning of words,
The wise woman who knows the meaning of dreams:
"My sister, listen, listen to my dream—
In my dream, rushes rise about me.
A single-growing reed trembles before me;
From a double-growing reed, first one,
then the other, is removed.
Water is poured on the holy hearth,
The bottom of my churn drops away,
My drinking cup falls from its peg.

The churn lies silent; no milk is poured;
The cup lies shattered—"

Geshtinanna spoke:
"O brother, do not tell me such a dream.
The rushes which rise about you are your *galla;*
They will pursue and attack you.
The single-growing reed which trembles before you
Is our mother. She will mourn for you.
The double-growing reed is you and I, Dumuzi,
First one, then the other, will be taken away.

When the fire is put out on your holy hearth,
The sheepfold will become a house of desolation.
When the bottom of your churn drops away,
Your *galla* will seize you.
When your drinking cup falls from its peg,
You will fall to the earth, to your mother's knees.
O brother, do not tell me such a dream—"

Dumuzi cried:

"Sister, quickly! I hear them!
Do not go with slow noble steps.
Sister, run! Go up the hill!
The *galla,* hated and feared by all
Are coming on boats.
Sister, run—"

Geshtinanna ran up the hill.
Dumuzi's friend went with her.
Dumuzi cried:

"Do you see them?"

Geshtinanna and Dumuzi's friend cried:

"They are coming! Your *galla* are coming!
They carry wood to bind the neck.
Brother, hide! Dumuzi, hide!!"

Dumuzi said:

"My sister, tell no one my hiding place.
My friend, tell no one my hiding place."

The *galla,* who have no sister, brother, wife, or child,
Who flutter over heaven and earth like wardens,
Who accept no favors, who cling to a man's side,
Went to the house of Geshtinanna and said:

"Show us where your brother is!"

Geshtinanna would not speak.

They offered her the grain gift, the fields in harvest.
She refused it.
They offered her the water gift, the river in its fullness.
She refused it.

Heaven was brought close.
Earth was brought close.
She would not speak.

They tore her clothes.
They poured pitch into her vulva.
She would not speak.

The *galla* went to the house of Dumuzi's friend.
They offered him the grain gift, the fields in harvest.
He accepted it.
They offered him the water gift, the river in its fullness.
He accepted it. He said:
"Dumuzi hid in the ditches of Arali."

The *galla* found Dumuzi in the ditches of Arali.
The *galla* bound his hands. They bound his neck.
They beat the husband of Inanna.
Dumuzi raised his arms to Utu, the Sun God, and cried:
"Utu, you are a just god, I am the husband of your sister!
I carried food to the holy shrine,
I kissed the holy lips,
I danced on the holy knees, the knees of Inanna.
Change my hands to gazelle hands,
Change my feet to gazelle feet,
Do not let them hold me."

The merciful Utu accepted Dumuzi's tears.
He changed Dumuzi's hands to gazelle hands.
He changed Dumuzi's feet to gazelle feet.
Dumuzi escaped.

He fled to Kubiresh,
The *galla* fled to Kubiresh.

He fled to Old Belili,
The *galla* fled to Old Belili.

He fled to the sheepfold of his sister, Geshtinanna.

When Geshtinanna found Dumuzi in the sheepfold, she wept.
She brought her mouth close to heaven.
She brought her mouth close to earth.
Her grief covered the horizon like a garment.

The *galla* climbed the reed fence.
The first *galla* struck Dumuzi in the cheek with a piercing nail,
The second *galla* struck his other cheek with a shepherd's crook,
The third *galla* smashed the bottom of his churn,
The fourth *galla* threw his drinking cup down from its peg,
The fifth *galla* shattered the churn,
The sixth *galla* shattered the cup,
The seventh *galla* cried:
"Rise, Dumuzi! Rise from your false sleep!
Husband of Inanna, son of Sirtur,
brother of Geshtinanna!
Your ewes are seized. Your lambs are seized!
Your goats are seized. Your kids are seized!

Take off your crown from your head!
Take off your royal garments from your body!
Take off your sandals from your feet!
Naked you go with us!"

They seized Dumuzi.
They bound his hands. They bound his feet.
They took him away.

The churn lies silent. No milk is poured.
The cup lies shattered. Dumuzi is no more.
The sheepfold is given to the winds.

In the city, the people wept for Dumuzi:
Dumuzi is taken captive in Uruk.
"He will no longer bathe in Eridu.
He will no longer treat the mother of Inanna
as his mother.
He will no longer raise his sword high."

Inanna mourned for Dumuzi:
"Gone is my husband, my sweet husband.
Gone is my love, my sweet love.
The wild bull lives no more.

O you flies of the steppe,
My beloved has been taken from the city.
Dumuzi has been taken from me
Before I could wrap him with a proper shroud.

I ask the hills and valleys:
'Where is my husband?'

I say to them:
'I can no longer bring him food:
I can no longer bring him drink.
The shepherd lives no more.'

The jackal lies down in his bed.
The raven now dwells in his sheepfold.
You ask me for his reed pipe?
The wind must play it for him.
You ask me for his sweet songs?
The wind must sing them for him."

Sirtur, the mother of Dumuzi, wandered across the steppe.
She wept for her son:

"My heart plays the reed pipe of sorrow.
Once my child wandered freely on the steppe,
Now he cannot move his hands.
He cannot move his feet.
The ewe gives up her lamb.
The goat gives up her kid.
My heart plays the reed pipe of sorrow.

O treacherous steppe, where is my child?
I would go to him.
I would see his face."

The mother walked to the desolate place.
She walked to where Dumuzi lay.
She looked at the slain wild bull.
She looked into his face. She said:

"My child, the face is yours.
The spirit has fled."

There is sorrow in the house.
There is grief in the inner chambers.

Geshtinanna wandered through the streets of the city,
Weeping for her brother:

"O my brother, who is your sister?
I am your sister.

O Dumuzi, who is your mother?
I am your mother.
The day that dawns for you will also dawn for me.
The day that you will see I will also see.

I would go to you,
I would comfort you,
I would share your fate."

When Inanna saw the grief of Geshtinanna, she said:
"Dumuzi has been taken away.
I would take you to him
But I do not know the place."

Then a holy fly appeared.
It circled the head of Inanna and spoke:
"If I tell you where Dumuzi is,
What will you give me?"

Inanna said:
"I will let you dwell in the beer-houses and taverns
Among the talk of the wise ones and the songs
of the minstrels."

The fly said:
"Then lift your eyes to the edges of the steppe,
Lift your eyes to Arali.
There you will find Geshtinanna's brother,
There you will find the shepherd Dumuzi."

Inanna and Geshtinanna went to the edges of the steppe.
They found Dumuzi, weeping.

Inanna took Dumuzi by the hand and said:
"You will go to the underworld half the year.
Your sister, since she has asked,
Will go the other half.
On the day you are called,
That day you will be taken.
On the day your sister is called,
That day you will be set free."

Inanna placed Dumuzi in the hands of the eternal.

The people of Sumer assemble in the palace,
The house which guides the land.
The king builds a throne for the queen of the palace.
He sits beside her on the throne.

In order to care for the life of all the lands,
The exact first day of the month is closely examined;
And, on the day of the disappearance of the moon,
The *me* are perfectly carried out
So that the New Year's Day, the day of rites,
May be properly determined,
And a sleeping place be set up for Inanna.

The people cleanse the rushes with sweet-smelling
cedar oil.
They arrange the rushes for the bed.
They spread a bridal sheet on the bed.
A bridal sheet to rejoice the heart,
A bridal sheet to sweeten the loins,
A bridal sheet for Inanna and Dumuzi.

Inanna bathes for the shepherd Dumuzi,
She washes herself with soap,
She sprinkles sweet-smelling cedar oil on the ground.
Dumuzi goes with lifted head to the sweet loins,
He lies down beside Inanna on the bed.
Tenderly caressing her, he murmurs words of love:
"O my holy jewel! O my wondrous Inanna!"

After Dumuzi enters her
Causing Inanna to rejoice,
Inanna holds him to her and says:
"Dumuzi, you are truly my love."

The king invites the people to enter the great hall.
The people bring food offerings and bowls.
They burn juniper resin.
They perform laving rites and pile up
sweet-smelling incense.

Inanna, seated on the royal throne, shines like daylight.
Dumuzi, like the sun, shines radiantly by her side.
He arranges abundance, lushness, and plenty before her.
He assembles the people of Sumer.

The musicians play for the queen:
They play the loud instrument which drowns out
the southern storm,
They play the sweet *algar* instrument, the ornament
of the palace,
They play the stringed instrument.
They celebrate Inanna in song.

Dumuzi reaches out his hand for food and drink.
The palace is festive. The king is joyous.
Dumuzi hails Inanna with the praises of the gods
    and the assembly:
        "Holy Priestess! Created with the heavens and the earth,
        First Daughter of the Moon, Lady of the Evening!
        I sing your praises."

Inanna looks in sweet wonder from heaven.
The people of Sumer parade before the holy Inanna.
The Lady Who Ascends into the Heavens, Inanna, is radiant.
Mighty, majestic, radiant, and ever youthful—
To you, Inanna, I sing.

SHIVA AND SATI

The Eternal Dance of the Universe

In memory of Joseph Campbell and Erlo Van Waveren

The Creator Brahma sat in serene meditation. Around him in a circle stood his ten sons, the ten world guardians, and Daksha. They watched as Brahma sank into himself, and with each vision an apparition appeared in bodily form.

Then Brahma plunged suddenly into the depths of his own darkness, and to the surprise of the assembly there stood a young, beautiful, naked woman. She was Dawn. She had a face as round as the moon, glistening blue-black hair, eyes like dark lotuses, and upturned, dark-tipped breasts.

The assembly stared at her in astonishment. She, in turn, laughed a soft rippling laugh which brought Brahma out of his trance so that he wondered, as did all who gazed at her, for what purpose in the unfolding of the creation this amazing apparition might have been summoned.

Then, a second surprise. From Brahma's wonder another creature came into being. He was Desire—a dark, strong, splendid youth, with beautifully formed limbs and an aroma of blossoms. In one hand he carried a banner with the emblem of a fish; in the other, a bow and five flowery arrows. As Brahma and his ten mindborn sons and the ten world guardians stared at the youth, desire crept into each of them, the desire to possess the radiant woman Dawn.

The moment Desire entered the world, he turned and spoke boldly to Brahma, "What is my name? And what am I to do? Each being flourishes when doing the work for which he is designed. Give me my name, and since you are a Creator, give me a wife!"

Brahma was silent for a moment. What had he done? Who was this creature who had slipped from his being? Brahma gathered his consciousness and brought his being to center. And because he was Brahma, the divine original consciousness, he spoke the truth, even if it meant that his own powers might be lessened.

"You will wander the earth with your bow," Brahma said. "And no creature will be able to escape the aim of your arrows. Your task will be to send your arrows into the hearts of men, women, and gods, causing bewilderment and delight, thus assuring the continual creation of the world."

Then Daksha, the lord of the ten world guardians, said to the youth, "Your name is Kama, God of Love, and your arrows will be stronger than those of Brahma, Vishnu, and even Shiva. You are the All-Pervader. We are all in your power."

When Kama heard these words, he turned to the gods, drew his bow taut, and let his arrows fly.

Intoxicating breezes permeated the assembly. Heavy scents of spring flowers brought rapture. The gods stumbled. They reeled from side to side. They stared at the woman Dawn. They gaped. They groaned. One by one, they went mad. Brahma broke into a sweat. Daksha and the world guardians began to quiver. . . .

The quivering and shaking caused a rumbling in the firmament, and in the far distant mountains, Shiva, the ascetic of the universe, was disturbed in his concentration. He drifted toward the Love Constellation, and when he saw the infatuated Brahma and his gaping flock, he burst into laughter.

"Well, well! And what is all this? Brahma, have you forgotten that you yourself revealed the laws of the Rig Vedas, 'The sister shall be as the mother and the daughter shall be as the sister'? The universe is founded on constancy. How can you permit yourself to lose your balance at the mere sight of a woman?"

At these words Brahma's mind split in two. He returned to his True Being; yet a part of him was still gripped by desire and lust. Waves of heat streamed down Brahma's limbs. Sweat poured down the bodies of the world guardians. From Daksha's sweat a splendid woman, gleaming like burnished gold, appeared. Daksha gave her to Kama as a wife and called this first wife Rati, which means delight.

At last Brahma was cleansed of his lust. Shiva then withdrew to his place of meditation, but the sting of Shiva's words did not leave Brahma. Brahma had been rebuked before his holy sons. He burned with humiliation.

"Why is it that Shiva is not moved by a woman?" he fumed. "If Shiva continues to remain aloof from all the universe, how will he be able to carry out his appointed tasks? If he remains forever in a rocklike state of meditation, how will he be able to destroy the enemies of the earth when a renewal is necessary?"

As Brahma came out of his meditations, he saw the young God of Love, Kama, joyfully united with his beautiful Rati and he said to them, "How blissful and radiant you are. What joy there is in seeing you together. You must go to the mountain tops where Shiva lives and set him on fire with love, so that he too may take a wife and join us in the eternal dance of the universe."

Kama answered, "If you order it, I will go. But if I succeed in stirring the rocklike Shiva, where is there a woman who can rouse him? Nowhere do I see such a woman for Shiva."

"I shall create her," Brahma replied. "Now go."

When Kama had departed, Brahma spoke with Daksha and said, "Who can Shiva's future wife be? What possible woman does he hold in the depths of his spirit? Yet, there is only one. Maya, the World Illusion, the Enchantress, Shakti, the Energy of the World. She can take any form. She is the one who will beguile him. Daksha, you must go and with proper offerings persuade Shakti to be born as your daughter and then to become Shiva's bride."

Daksha understood the wisdom of Brahma's suggestion and took himself to the other side of the divine Milky Ocean, across the timeless sea where Vishnu sleeps and dreams the dream of the world. There he prepared himself to make offerings to the great goddess who is the manifestation of Vishnu's dream. With the image of the Enchantress in his mind and heart, he went into deep meditation so that by his heat he could animate her image and see the goddess with his own eyes. For 36,000 years Daksha remained in a state of prolonged concentration, creating his vision of the goddess.

While Daksha sat meditating, the mighty Brahma went to the holy mountain, Mandara. And there, for 36,000 years, he praised with potent syllables the Mother of the Universe. He called to Shakti in her myriad forms:

"Maya, Goddess beyond Reach, Enchantress, Everlasting Divine Drunkenness of Dream, Lady of the Spheres, Smoky One, Weaver of the World, Wisdom, Compassion, Delusion, Daughter of the Mountain, Earth-born, Youngest One, Golden One, Peace of the Night, Mother of the World, Giver of Food, Shining One, Wanton-Eyed, Auspicious, One Who Releases, Three-Eyed . . ."

At the end of 36,000 years, Maya appeared, standing on the back of her tawny lion. She was dark and slender with her hair hanging freely.

Brahma greeted her, "O Kali, Dark One. I have called to you because of your power. The Lord of Spirits, Shiva, remains solitary. If he takes no wife, the creation of the world will not continue in its appointed course. Only you can entice and bewitch him into the eternal dance of the universe—"

Kali answered, "What you say is true. I am the Divine Energy of the Universe. From me comes the food of the universe, all that has breath, all that speaks. I make each one what he or she wishes to be—great and powerful, weak and helpless, passionate, full of dreams. For the sake of the creation, I will agree to entice Shiva. When Shiva meditates and goes into the innermost kernel of his heart, he will find me there. I will have melted into his heart."

She disappeared. And on the other side of time, Daksha saw the goddess and she reappeared to him on her lion. Her body was dark, her breasts were mighty. Daksha bowed to her and announced his wish. She answered, "For the sake of the well-being of creation, I will grant your wish. I will become your daughter and the wife of Shiva. But if for a single moment you lose proper reverence for me, I will not remain on earth. I will leave my body, whether I am happy or not."

Daksha returned to earth, full of joy that his wish had been granted. He married a beautiful woman, Virani, the daughter of Virana, the fragrant grass. Virani conceived at once from the vision of Daksha's soul.

When the child was born and she was a girl, flowers descended from the heavens. Virani did not know that her daughter was Maya, the Mother of the Universe, the Great Enchantress. She only knew a little infant was wailing, and she took the child in her arms and gave her her breast to suck.

The child grew. When she played with her small friends, she delighted in drawing pictures of Shiva, and when she sang, her childlike songs were of her love for Shiva. Shiva was always in her heart. Her father gave her the most beautiful name. He called her Sati, which means "She Who Is."

When she became a young woman, she went to the mountains to meditate. Then Brahma, with his divine wife, Savitri, and Vishnu, with his divine wife, Lakshmi, went to visit Shiva in his place of peace. When Shiva saw them, a strange thing happened. The Paragon of Peace was moved by the radiance and bliss in the faces of the two joyous couples, and the smallest trace of desire for a woman entered his heart.

"We have come to you," Brahma said, "for the sake of the creation. I am the Creator, Vishnu is the Preserver, and you are the Destroyer. But if you remain in your state of rocklike meditation, how will you understand passion and be able to destroy when the moment for destruction arrives? We have come for the sake of creation to ask you to take a wife."

Shiva said, "At every moment I see the supreme eternity of the True Being. At every moment I keep it before me. Where is the woman who is as consecrated to my work as I am and as dedicated to the Highest Vision? If, for the sake of the universe, I were to take a wife, where is there a woman who would be capable of absorbing my incandescent power, shock by shock?"

Brahma was elated. He said, "She exists! At this moment, she is waiting for you and longing for you! Her name is Sati!"

The two couples left Shiva.

Shiva descended to earth to the place where Sati was meditating alone in the mountains. When she opened her eyes and saw Shiva standing before her, she was flooded with joy. She fell to the ground and worshiped his feet.

When Shiva saw Sati, he was pleased. "What do you wish?" he asked. "Speak."

But Sati could not utter a word. She could not speak before the one who had moved her heart since she was a child.

Shiva was filled with longing to hear her voice, and at that very moment, Kama, the God of Love, drew his arrow and shot Shiva through the heart. Shiva shuddered. He forgot his True Being and cried, "Be my wife!"

Sati, frightened by the great god, trembled and said, "Speak to my father." Then she ran toward her home.

Shiva, the Paragon of Peace, returned to his mountain abode. He directed his thoughts toward Brahma and Brahma appeared.

"Brahma," he said, "you have won. I am powerless. Maya has caught me in her web. Now all I can be, all I can become, is Sati's husband. You must arrange it. Brahma, speak to Daksha, ask him if he will permit me to marry Sati."

So the wedding of Shiva and Sati was arranged. It was held on the day and at the hour that was most propitious according to the stars.

The bridegroom, Shiva, arrived, accompanied by divine musicians and dancing girls. He wore a loincloth of tiger skins and, for decoration, a live serpent draped from his left shoulder to his right hip. In his hair rested the young moon and a garland of skulls.

The lesser and greater spirits, all incarnations of the great Shiva, danced. The dancing girls danced. Flowers poured down from the heavens. Kama delighted Shiva and maddened him. The whole firmament was gay and brilliant, blown with sweet-scented breezes. All the trees were in blossom.

Solemnly, Shiva received Sati's hand. The gods gave praise, reciting the verses from the holy Vedas. Then Vishnu spoke and blessed Shiva and Sati, saying:

"Sati gleams blue-black and Shiva is fair. Together you will protect gods and mortals. Shiva, you will slay the enemies as they arise in the course of history, and if anyone lets his desire rest on Sati, you will destroy that one without a thought."

"So be it!" said Shiva. And Sati laughed a joyous, merry laugh.

Her laughter caught the ear of Brahma, and Brahma turned and looked at Sati. The God of Love entered his veins and Brahma began to smoke with desire for Sati. Great energy in the form of flames and fire streamed out of Brahma's body, and a black thundercloud spread out over the earth stretching to the rim of the world. Brahma could not take his eyes from Sati. The holy assembly stared at Brahma in horror.

When Shiva saw how Brahma's eyes feasted on Sati, he cried out, "I shall kill you!" He lifted his spear to throw at Brahma, but Vishnu quickly rushed between them and held Shiva's arm.

"You can not kill the Creator of the World," Vishnu said. "He is the one who created Sati. Brahma is the one who prepared her for you."

"I will keep my vow!" Shiva cried. "I will create another Creator, but no one will look at Sati like that. Let me go. Take away your hand."

But Vishnu said, "You may not kill the Creator. He is yourself. You and he are one."

"What are you saying?" Shiva asked. "Everyone can see I am Shiva and that is Brahma."

Vishnu said, "Maya has tricked you and you no longer see your True Being. Close your eyes," he said to Shiva, "so that you may find your center."

And before the holy assembly, Shiva closed his eyes and sank into himself. His body began to glow, and the light was so dazzling no one could look. Maya withdrew from his body. Then Vishnu, like the light of heaven, poured into the body of Shiva and showed him the procession and history of the world:

At first, all was darkness.
There was nothing.
No day or night,
heaven or earth.

There was time.
Time unfolded
in the great cosmic egg,
the egg which grew in the waters
enveloped by winds and flame and space.
Inside the egg,
Shiva saw the Creator,
white as a white lotus,
streaming white,
and the Creator was opening up the world.

The Creator began to divide:
the top part was Brahma,
the middle dark blue part was Vishnu,
and the crystalline underpart was Shiva.
They melted from one to another.
The three grew out of each other;
they flowed into each other
and the egg rocked in the water
and burst open
and the shell arranged itself into bounding mountains;
Shiva became distinct from Brahma
and from Vishnu.

Then Shiva saw Kama and the holy ones,
the sun, the moon, the clouds; the fish, the turtles,
the monsters and men;
and then he saw the most beautiful woman of all.
She was Sati.

And then he saw how Maya,
in the figure of Lakshmi, was enchanting Vishnu
and how Maya, in the figure of Savitri
    was enchanting Brahma,
even while he was enchanted by Sati.

And he saw the future.
He saw Sati and himself on a mountain pinnacle
enlaced in love.
He saw Sati take off her body
and disappear and be born again
as the daughter of Menaka, Queen of the Mountain.
After a long separation,
he found her and
they were joined together again.

All this Shiva saw in an instant. Then Vishnu withdrew from Shiva's body, and Shiva came out of his trance. All he could see was the lovely Sati. He lifted Sati onto his white bull, Nandi, and they rode to the tops of the Himalayan peaks. There they dwelt and there they played, night and day, and all their play was love.

Shiva went and gathered wildflowers for Sati. He let down her night-dark hair and played with it. Then he knotted it up so that he might loosen it again. He painted her pretty feet with scarlet lac so that he might hold them in his hands, and he whispered in her ear what he might have said aloud, but in this way he could be closer to her.

In the bowers and by the banks of high mountain streams, they tasted each other and played with each other and loved each other. Shiva put a spot of musk on Sati's beautiful lotus breasts and lifted off her necklaces of pearl and set them back again just to touch her lotus softness. He drew off her bracelets and opened the knots of her clothing and tied them back again. He decked her whole body with chains of flowers and swallowed the nectar of her mouth and their desire for each other never ceased. The fountain of their passion was fed by their love. And so they loved, and 9,000 years passed quickly by.

It then happened that Daksha, Sati's father, decided to hold a Great Offering to the Supreme Being. He invited every living being in all the reaches of space: the gods and demons, the spirits, the clouds and mountains, the rivers and oceans, the mortals, beasts, and birds, the trees and grasses. Shiva and Sati were the only two creatures in the universe that he did not invite.

He thought that Shiva, who meditates among corpses and carries a skull for a begging bowl, would not be a fitting guest to attend such an offering. And, of course, he could not invite his beloved daughter Sati if he did not invite her husband.

Vijaya, the daughter of the sister of Sati, went to visit Sati. Shiva had gone off on his bull, Nandi, to perform his evening meditations and Sati was alone.

"Dear Vijaya," Sati said, "you have come by yourself. Where are your sisters?"

"They are preparing for the great celebration. All the women in the universe are preparing themselves. I have come to bring you—are you and Shiva not coming?"

"What celebration? Where?"

"Oh Sati! Have you not been invited? Your father, Daksha, is holding a Great Offering. Everyone in all the worlds has been invited."

Sati was struck as if she had been hit by a bolt of lightning. Anger began to burn in her and her eyes hardened. She said, "It is because my husband carries a skull for a begging bowl."

And she thought to blast Daksha to ashes with a curse. But then she remembered her words to Daksha, "If for a single moment, you lose proper reverence for me, I will not remain. I will leave my body, whether I am happy or not."

As Sati's eternal form became visible to her, she thought, "I will leave this body. I will not stay. The gods will not have what they wish this time. But one day I will return to Mount Himalaya where I have dwelt so long in happiness with Shiva, and there I will be born as the daughter of Menaka. I will play and then I will marry Shiva and complete the work the gods have wished for."

With that, she closed the nine portals of her body. She withdrew her breath and braced herself. Her life force shot up through her body and ripped through the top of her skull. Her body slumped to the ground.

When the gods above saw this, they lifted a universal cry of horror. Vijaya cried, "Oh Sati! Sati! What have I done? What have I said to hurt you? Your poor mother will be shattered by the pain. And how will your heartless father survive? Oh Sati, you were a mother to me. Sati, I am crying. Oh Sati, who will care for Shiva? *Shiva! OOH!*"

In his meditations Shiva heard Vijaya's shriek. He returned at once to their mountaintop where his beloved Sati lay crumbled on the earth. But love would not allow him to believe she was dead.

Gently, he stroked her cheek. "You are asleep?" he asked. "Love, what has sent you to sleep? Sati, wake up, speak!"

Then Vijaya told Shiva that something inside of Sati seemed to have burst when she was told that neither she nor Shiva had been invited to the Great Offering Daksha was giving.

Shiva's whole being was filled with wrath. He transported himself to the place where the Great Sacrifice was being held. There he saw the living creatures who had been invited: the gods, the planets, the beasts, the fish, the worms, the seasons, the ages of the world, and each was reverently carrying out his role. Only he and Sati had not been invited.

Shiva stepped into the sacred place to destroy the offering. At the sight of Shiva, the young animal that was about to be sacrificed transformed itself into a gazelle and fled to the heavens. Shiva followed and the gazelle found refuge in Brahma's realm. Shiva followed and the gazelle fled to Vishnu's realm. Shiva followed. At last, the frightened animal darted back to earth and disappeared on a mountaintop, hiding itself in Sati's corpse.

When Shiva stood once again before the corpse of Sati, he forgot the offering. He saw only Sati. And then a great cry of grief came from his throat and his heart broke.

He looked at Sati—at her lips, her cheeks, her beautiful dark hair. Then her laughter, her kindness, her touch rushed through him and he broke with grief like a common mortal.

He flung himself on the ground. He crouched by her corpse. He got up and ran and returned and reached out and touched her body. It was stiff and cold. He caressed her forehead and cheeks and lips. He undid her clothing and then fastened it again. He picked Sati up in his arms and began to walk. He sobbed and walked and sobbed and he would not let her go.

Vishnu and Brahma watched Shiva, and they knew that Sati's corpse would never decay as long as Shiva held her. And so by their craft, Brahma and Vishnu hid in Sati's corpse, and as Shiva walked, they dismembered Sati's body.

Her two feet fell, and the place that they fell was called the Mountain of the Goddess. Not far from there her two ankles fell. And then to the east her womb fell and, nearby, her navel; then her two breasts together with her gold necklace, and her shoulders, and her neck. Every place a part of her fell became a sacred place and a blessing to the children of the world.

When her head fell, Shiva stopped. He stood and stared and broke into a terrible groan of pain.

The gods at once gathered around Shiva and wished to comfort him. But Shiva was ashamed and transformed himself into a rock in the shape of a lingam.

The gods praised Shiva, hoping he would return to himself. "Light of all Lights, in your form of lingam you are the Highest Being. You understand the impermanence of all things. Shiva, we tremble before your grief. Shiva, let your anguish pass! Shiva!"

Shiva remembered his Highest Self, which had always been the object of his meditations, but he could not bring his powers into focus. His grief was overwhelming.

Shiva opened his eyes. He saw Brahma and said, "Brahma, what am I to do?"

And Brahma answered, "You must let your pain go. You must let your anguish go. It is only Maya. Return to your True Being. In the eternal dance of the universe you will find Sati again."

And Shiva said, "Brahma, I can do nothing. Brahma, stay with me until the pain passes, until I come up from the ocean of my loss. Do not leave me, Brahma. Stay with me and give me comfort."

And Brahma said, "So be it."

Blind with suffering, Shiva took Brahma's hand and the two gods departed into the solitude of the mountains. They walked until they came to a lake. It was surrounded by holy hermits who were meditating. The lake was clear, quiet, and peaceful.

Shiva sat by the lake and looked into the waters. He saw fish swimming, darting in and out among the lotus stems. Beside the waters of this lake, Shiva found his rest. He released himself from his fixation. He released himself from his suffering and centered himself in the eternity of his True Being.

Shiva remained in deep peace and meditation until Sati was reborn as Parvati, the daughter of Menaka, Queen of the Mountain. By her long, sustained meditations, Parvati was able to stir Shiva from his deep place of peace and bring him to her, so that they were united in love.

Once again, the rebirth of the world was assured.

THE SONG OF SONGS

"Take me with you—and we will run!"

For Igor and Sonja Sudarsky

The Song of Songs which is Solomon's:

She:

Let him kiss me with the kisses of your mouth,
for your love is more wonderful than wine.
The oils of your body are fragrant.
The sound of your name is perfume.
No wonder the young women love you.
Take me with you—and we will run!

The king brings me into his chambers.
We will delight and rejoice in you,
sipping our fragrant love, rather than wine.
With good reason the young women love you.

I am black and beautiful, O women of Jerusalem,
like the goathair tents of Kedar
and the silk pavilions of Solomon.
Do not stare at me because I am so dark.
It was the sun that shone on me, burning me.
My mother's sons became angry with me
and set me to work guarding their vineyards;
but my own vineyard, I did not keep.

She:

Tell me, my love,
where do you feed your flock?
Where does your flock rest at noon?
Tell me, so I do not wander aimlessly
among the flocks of your companions.

He:

Most beautiful woman, if you do not know,
follow the tracks of the sheep
and let your lambs graze near the tents of the shepherds.

O woman, I shall compare you to a mare
among the chariots of Pharaoh.
Your cheeks are lovely under your sparkling bangles.
Your neck glitters with strings of beads.
We will make you bangles of gold
with droplets of silver.

She:

While the king rests on his bed,
my perfume gives off its fragrance.
My lover is like a bag of myrrh
lying between my breasts.
My beloved is like a cluster of henna
plucked from the vineyards of Ein Gedi.

He:

You are beautiful, my love.
You are beautiful.
Your eyes are doves.

She:

O love, it is you
who are beautiful,
you who are radiant.
Our bed is fresh and green.
The beams of our house are cedar
and the rafters are cypress.

She:

I am a crocus growing on the plains.
I am a lily growing in the valleys.

He:

My love among the young women
is like a lily among the thistles.

She:

My love among the young men
is like an apple tree among the trees of the forest.
I long to sit in his shade
and to taste his sweet fruit on my palate.

He brings me into his vineyard.
His banner of love flies over me.
O, my beloved, feed me with raisin cakes,
sustain me with apples,
for I am faint with love.

She:

Let his left hand lie under my head
and his right hand caress me.
Young women of Jerusalem, swear to me,
by the gazelles and does of the field,
that you will not arouse or stir love
until love is ready to awake.

She:

Listen! Do you hear? It is the voice of my love.
Here he comes,
leaping over the mountains,
bounding over the hills.
My love is like a buck,
like a young stag.

He is here,
standing behind our wall.
He looks through the window.
He peers through the lattices.
He raises his voice and calls to me.

He:

Rise, my love, my lovely one, and come away with me.
The winter is past,
The rains are gone,
The buds appear on the earth.
The time for singing has come.

The voice of the dove is heard in the land.
The fig trees form their first fruits.
The blossoming vines give off their fragrance.
Rise, my love, my lovely one, and come away with me!

O, my dove, in the clefts of the cliff,
in the secret places of the rock,
let me see your face;
let me hear your voice;
for your voice is clear
and your face is beautiful.

She:

Young women of Jerusalem, catch the foxes—
the little foxes who spoil the vineyard;
for our vineyard has just come into blossom.
My love is mine
and I am his.
He feeds among the lilies.

When the evening winds arise
and the shadows flee,
return, my love,
and be like a buck or a young stag
on the mountain of spices.

She:

At night on my bed,
I sought the one my soul loves.
I looked for him, but I did not find him.

I shall get up now and go about the city
into the streets and open places
searching for the one my soul loves.

I asked for him, but I did not find him.
The watchmen who go about the city found me.
"Have you seen him? Have you seen my love?" I asked.

A moment after they passed, I found him,
and when I found him I seized him
and I would not let him go
until I brought him into my mother's house
and into the bedroom of the one who conceived me.

Young women of Jerusalem, swear to me,
by the gazelles and the does of the field,
that you will not arouse or stir love
until love is ready to awake.

The Women:

Who is she who comes up from the wilderness
surrounded by pillars of smoke,
perfumed with myrrh and frankincense
and all the powders of the peddlers?

Look! Look well!
It is the bed of Solomon, escorted by sixty warriors.
Sixty of the mighty warriors of Israel surround the bed.
Each one is skilled in battle,
yet each one carries a sword on his thigh
to protect him from the terrors of the night.

From the trees of Lebanon
King Solomon had a palanquin made.

Its posts are of silver.
The headboard is of gold.
The cushions are purple wool
and the insides are embroidered with the love
of the young women of Jerusalem.

Come, young women of Zion, come out!
Come and look at King Solomon
He is wearing the crown
his mother crowned him with on his wedding day,
the day of the great joy of his heart.

He:

My love, you are beautiful.
You are truly beautiful.
Your eyes are doves behind your veil.
Your hair is like a flock of goats
streaming down the side of Mount Gilead.
Your teeth are like two rows of sheep
coming up from the washing.
Each one has a twin
and not one is alone.
Your lips are a thread of scarlet wool.
Your mouth is lovely.
Your brow is a fresh slice of pomegranate
shining through your veil.
Your neck is like David's tower.
The strands of your necklaces are placed one upon another.
From the beads of your necklaces hang a thousand shields
belonging to the mighty warriors.
Your breasts are like two fawns,
twins of a gazelle,
browsing among the lilies.

He:

When the evening winds arise
and the shadows flee,
I shall return to the mountain of myrrh
and the hill of frankincense.
My love, you are beautiful.
There is no blemish in you.

He:

My bride, come with me from Lebanon.
Come with me from Lebanon. Come! Come now!
We will leap from the peak of Amon,
from the peaks of Senir and Hermon,
passing dens of lions
and mountains of panthers.

My sister, my bride, you have ravished my heart.
You have ravished my soul
with one glance of your eye,
with one bead of your necklace.

My bride, your breasts are beautiful.
Your caress, my sister, is more wonderful than wine,
and your scent more fragrant than any spice.

Your lips drip honey, my bride.
Honey and milk lie under your tongue,
and the fragrance of your dress
is the fragrance of Lebanon.

A closed garden is my sister, my bride.
A closed well.
A sealed fountain.

Your plants form an orchard of pomegranates,
laden with ripe fruit and sweet spices—
henna and nard, nard and saffron,
calamus and cinnamon,
branches of incense, myrrh, aloes—all the sweetest spices.
The well in your garden
is a fountain of living waters
rushing down from Lebanon.

She:

O north wind, awake.
South wind, rise up.
Blow on my garden
and let my spices flow.
Let my love enter his garden
and eat his sweet fruit.

He:

My sister, my bride, I have entered my garden.
I have gathered my myrrh with my spices.
I have eaten my honeycomb with my honey.
I have drunk my wine with my milk.
Eat, friends, drink! And become drunk with love!

She:

I was sleeping, but my heart was awake.
Listen . . . my love is knocking at the door.

He:

Let me in, my sister, my friend, my dove, my perfect one.
Let me in, for my head is drenched with dew
and my hair is damp with the night mist.

She:

I have taken off my dress.
Shall I put it on again?
I have washed my feet.
Shall I soil them again?

My love thrust his hand
into the opening in the door,
and my insides quivered.
I got up to open the door
and my hands dripped myrrh.
My fingers were flowing myrrh
on the bars of the door.

I opened for my love,
but he had turned and gone away.
My soul fainted when I remembered
the words he had spoken.

I searched for him, but I did not find him.
I called to him, but he did not answer me.
The watchmen who go about the city found me.
They struck me—
they bruised me.
The guardians of the wall took my shawl from me.

Young women of Jerusalem, swear to me,
that if you find my beloved
you will tell him that I am faint with love.

The Women:
Most beautiful of women,
how is it that your beloved is so different from other men?
How is your lover so different that
you would make us swear like this?

She:
My love is shining and ruddy.
He is the tallest in a crowd of ten thousand men.
His head is like burnished gold.
His hair is black and curled like a raven's.
His eyes are like doves,
near pools of water,
washed with milk and brightly set.
His cheeks are like beds of spices,
banks of sweet-smelling herbs.
His lips are lilies,
dripping fragrant myrrh.
His arms are like rods of gold,
set with beryl.
His loins are the smoothest ivory,
adorned with sapphires.
His legs are pillars of marble
on foundations of gold.
He is as wondrous to look at
as the cedars of Lebanon.
His mouth is full of sweetness.
All of him is a delight.
He is my love.
He is my friend, O women of Jerusalem.

The Women:

Most beautiful of women,
where did your beloved go?
Where did he turn?
Tell us, so we can help you find him.

She:

My love has gone down to his garden,
to the beds of spices.
He has gone to feed in his garden
and to gather lilies.

I am his
and he is mine.
He feeds among the lilies.

He:

My beloved, you are as lovely as the green fields of Tirzah,
as radiant as Jerusalem,
as awesome as an army with great banners.
Turn your eyes away from me
for they overwhelm me.

Sixty are the queens.
Eighty are the concubines.
There are young women without number,
but one is my dove.
She is perfect,
She is her mother's only daughter,
She is her mother's favorite.
The young women who see her adore her,
The queens and concubines sing her praises.

Who is she who shines like the morning star,
as lovely as the moon,
as radiant as the sun,
and as awesome as an army with great banners?

She:

I went down to the walnut garden
to look at the first fruits of the valley,
to see if the grapevine was in blossom
and if the pomegranates were in flower.
And I do not know how it was
but my soul swooned
and I found myself in the chariot
next to my prince.

Chorus:

Turn, turn! Turn, O Shulamite!
Dance for us so we can gaze at you!

She:

And what will you see when you gaze at Shulamite
as she dances the Dance of the Two Armies?

Chorus:

O prince's daughter, how graceful are your feet in sandals.
The curves of your thighs are like ornaments
crafted by artists' hands.
Your womb is a moon-shaped goblet
never wanting for wine.
Your belly is a heap of wheat,
surrounded by lilies.
Your breasts are two fawns,
twins of a gazelle.

Your neck is like a tower of ivory.
Your eyes are like the pools of Heshbon,
by the gates of Bath-Rabbim.
Your nose is like the tower of Lebanon,
looking toward Damascus.
Your head sits upon you like Mount Carmel.
Your flowing hair is crimson.
The king is held captive in your tresses.
How beautiful you are! How lovely you are!
You are love in all its delights!

Your figure is like a palm tree
and your breasts are like clusters of dates.
I am thinking I shall climb that palm tree
and take hold of the branches.

Then your breasts will be as soft as grapes,
your breath as fragrant as apples,
and your kiss like spiced wine,
flowing smoothly,
stirring the sleeper's lips to speak.

She:

I belong to my beloved
and his longing is for me.

Come, my love, to the fields.
We will spend the night in the villages
waking at dawn to go to the vineyards.
We will see if the grapevines are in blossom,
if the first buds of the grapes have formed,
and if the pomegranates are in flower—
there, I will give you my love.

She:

All kinds of precious fruit wait at our door,
precious fruit, new and old,
which I have been storing for you.

If only you were my brother
who had nursed at the breasts of my mother,
I could kiss you when I met you on the street,
and no one would scorn me.
I could bring you—
I could lead you into my mother's house,
and you would teach me.
You would drink the spiced wine
from the juice of my pomegranates.

O let his left hand lie under my head
and his right hand caress me.
Young women of Jerusalem, swear to me
that you will not arouse or stir love
until love is ready to awake.

The Women:

Who is she
who comes up from the wilderness
leaning on her lover's arm?

She:

I woke you with love under the apple tree,
there where your mother conceived you,
there where she who gave birth to you conceived you.

Set me as a seal on your heart,
and as a seal on your arm,

for love is as strong as death.
Its passions are as cruel as the grave
and its flashes of fire are the very flame of God.

Many waters can not quench love,
nor can the floods sweep it away.
If a man were to give all of his wealth to buy love,
he would be laughed at and scorned.

The brothers:

We have a little sister,
and her breasts are not yet formed.
What shall we do for our sister
on the day that her suitors arrive?

If she is a wall,
we will build fine turrets of silver around her.
If she is a door,
we will enclose her in planks of cedar.

She:

I am a wall,
and my breasts are like towers.
I have found favor in my lover's eyes,
and I am at peace.

Solomon, you gave your vineyard at Baal Hamon
to your caretakers.
Each man had to pay for the fruit
one thousand pieces of silver.

O Solomon, I take care of my own vineyard.
Here are one thousand pieces of silver for you
and two hundred pieces of silver
for those who guarded your fruit.

He:

My love, you sit in your garden,
and your friends hear your voice.
Let me too hear your voice.

She:

Then make haste, my beloved,
and be like a buck or a young stag
on the mountain of spices.

PSYCHE AND EROS

Love's Quest Brings Joy

For Gioia Timpanelli

Apuleius' novel The Golden Ass *begins with the hero Lucius, a well-connected, rather superficial fellow, who journeys to Thessaly, hoping to learn the secrets and powers of magic. Attractive women throw themselves at him, and his voluptuous, somewhat dim-witted mistress helps him transform into an owl, but by mistake he is transformed into a donkey.*

As an ass, Lucius is tortured, burdened, and witnesses almost every form of human love (and betrayal) imaginable. In the end, he eats a rose, regains his human form, and chooses to undergo the arduous ritual of becoming a devotee of Isis and divine love.

In one of Lucius' most frightening adventures he is forced to carry a virgin bride to a robber's hideout. To quiet the terrified bride, an old hag tells her a fairy tale. In his form of an ass, Lucius overhears the tale of "Psyche and Eros."

In the west of Greece, there were a king and queen who had three beautiful daughters. The older two were lovely, and there are words to describe them, but because of the shortcomings of our human language, there are no words to describe the beauty of the youngest. Every day, citizens and strangers alike flocked in great numbers to the palace just to gaze at her. When they saw her, they were so overwhelmed by her beauty that they made the gesture of reverence reserved for the Goddess of Love herself. They pressed the forefinger and thumb of their right hand to their lips and threw her adoring kisses.

Stories soon spread to the neighboring cities and provinces. One story reported: A new goddess, born from the dark blue womb of the sea and nourished on the foam of the waves, has, in her great kindness, taken on human form so that all who wish to may gaze at her divinity. Another rumor claimed: Due to the conjunction of the stars, Venus has had a second birth, this time from the earth not the water, and this time, wonder of all wonders, the flowery virgin *is* a virgin!

Every day, the princess' fame traveled a little farther, so that stories of her beauty soon extended to far-distant provinces and islands, causing men to make long journeys over land and sea in order to gaze at the great wonder of their age.

No one sailed anymore to Paphos or Cnidos or Cythera to visit the shrines of the Goddess of Love. Venus' rites and ceremonies were neglected. Her couches were trampled on. No violets or roses garlanded her statues. Cold ash lay on her altars. The people turned from the goddess to the girl, and the princess' face became their shrine. Every morning as the princess walked down the street, crowds would follow her, throwing violets and roses and shouting, "Venus!" "Golden One!" "Glorious One!"

When the true Venus realized that the honors due to her were being given to a mortal girl, she shook her head and raged aloud, "Is it possible that I, the Mother of the Universe, I, who gave the spark of life to every living being, should be forgotten, while a mere mortal is worshiped in my name? Shall my name, which is registered in the divine Book of the Muses, be defiled with earthly matters? Shall I be grateful for the remnants of worship that are left to me by a mortal, who will someday die? Was that great contest in vain when Paris, whom Jupiter admires for his judgment, chose me over Hera and Athena as the most beautiful goddess? This girl, whoever she is, shall soon repent of having rejoiced over her illicit beauty and shall rue the day she was ever called Venus."

Venus sent for her winged son, Eros. Perhaps you've heard of the rascal? He's the one who, armed with flames and arrows, delights in causing scandals. At night, he runs from household to household, disturbing the most respectable of marriages. He conscientiously does whatever he's not supposed to do; and yet, he never seems to be punished. Not needing to instruct her son in the art of mischief, Venus, nevertheless, incited him by telling him the entire story of her outrage. Then she led him to the city where the princess lived and showed him the girl whose name was Psyche. Venus said, "I beg you, by the love you have for your mother, put your arrow in your bowstring, draw it back, and let it fly into the heart of that miserable girl so that she falls passionately in love with the vilest, the lowest, and the most disgusting of all creatures, one that all the world would find dreadful. Do this for me, my sweet, and I will be avenged and most grateful." She kissed him for a long time with open lips and then ran off to the sea.

She danced across the waves, and under her rosy feet the tossing waters calmed. The surface of the sea became smooth, and as if sensing her wishes, the sea people appeared. The daughters of Nereus sang in chorus. With them came Portunus with his rough blue beard, and his wife, Salacia, her bosom full of fish. Tiny Palaemon rode on a dolphin, and troops of prancing tritons spread out across the ocean. One noisily blew on a conch shell. Another held a silk parasol over Venus' head to protect her from the fierce sun, and a third swam ahead, holding up a mirror should Venus wish to admire herself. The others swam together under her chariot. Such was the band of attendants that accompanied Venus on her ocean voyage.

But there were no such pleasures to delight the princess Psyche. Although she was stared at and praised by all, no king, or prince, or even a commoner dared to ask her hand in marriage. Psyche was admired for her divine beauty in the way one might admire an exquisite marble statue. Her two older sisters, who were of moderate beauty, celebrated happy weddings and married kings of noble standing. But the virgin Psyche stayed at home and mourned her fate. She was miserable in body and spirit and began to hate the beauty which gave others such delight.

The father worried for his neglected daughter. He suspected the anger of the gods and journeyed to Miletus to seek the advice of the Oracle of Apollo. Outside the temple, he washed in a spring and sacrificed a goat. Carefully, starting with his right foot, he climbed the thirteen steps of the temple. He gave the priest a petition which asked where a husband was to be found for his daughter. The priest descended the stairs of the dark, vaulted tunnel and gave the king's petition to the Pythia. The Pythia purified herself and came out into the sunlit courtyard. She chewed on laurel leaves, inhaled the vapors from the sacred well, and fell into a trance. The words she spoke in Greek were later translated into Latin (for which both the author of this tale and the king were grateful):

King, bring your daughter to the mountaintop,
Dress her in funeral robes to meet her spouse.
A bridegroom he is, but not of mortal seed;
A winged creature, fierce and cruel,
Weakening all the world with his fire and sword.
He causes fear in the court of Jupiter
And terror in the Stygian shades.

When he heard the words of the Oracle, the once happy father sadly and reluctantly returned home. He told his wife the dreadful answer he had received, and the two mourned and wept for many days.

At last, the time came for the dreadful prophecy to be obeyed. A procession formed for Psyche's wedding. Torches burned with dark, sooty flames. Flutes did not play wedding tunes but sad Lydian laments. The wedding song ended with loud bursts of sorrow, and the bride wiped her tears with her wedding veil. The citizens of the city suspended their affairs to share the grief of the king and queen. A day of public mourning was ordered. Now the necessity of obeying the Oracle demanded that Psyche meet her fate.

Once the wedding vows were completed, the entire population, in great grief, followed Psyche, who walked as if she were attending a funeral rather than a wedding rite. Suddenly, Psyche's parents refused to go on. They could not bear the thought of their daughter's dreaded encounter and tried to delay the procession, but Psyche urged them on, saying, "Why do you torment yourselves in your old age with incessant wailing, weakening your spirits, which are dearer to me than my own? Why do you harm the faces I love, filling your eyes with tears and pulling out your gray hairs? Why do you pound the breasts that nourished me? Too late you understand the deadly blows of jealousy. Long ago, when the people celebrated us with divine reverence and called me the new Venus, that was the moment you should have wept, for that was the moment I became as one who is dead.

"Now I understand. I understand clearly: I am to perish because of the slanderous use of Venus' name. Lead me on. I want to lie on the rock which holds my fate. I hasten to my happy wedding and to my bridegroom. Why should I delay? Why should I fear him who can at his will destroy all the world?"

With resolute step, Psyche rejoined the procession. The people left her at the appointed rock, and started home in the darkness, with lowered heads, for their torches had been extinguished by their tears. The king and queen shut themselves in the palace. They closed the doors and windows and gave themselves up to unending grief.

On the highest rock, Psyche lay waiting and trembling. After a while, she felt the soft, gentle West Wind, Zephyrus. He rustled her skirts, growing stronger and stronger, until with a deep inhalation, he lifted her up into the air and carried her gently down, down to a green valley of fragrant flowers.

Psyche rested blissfully on a soft bed of tender grass. When she awoke, refreshed from her sweet sleep, she saw a dense grove of tall trees. In the middle of the grove was a fountain, and near the fountain a palace, one so magnificent that Psyche knew it could not have been made by mortal hands. From the very entrance it seemed to be the lodging of a god. The paneled ceilings were carved with lemonwood and ivory. The pillars were golden, and the walls were embossed with silver engravings of wild animals which seemed to be running toward her, as if to welcome her. Neither a man, nor even a demi-god, most likely only a god—could create such forms. The floor was a mosaic of precious gems forming patterns that changed at every glance. Anyone who walked on such a floor would surely be blessed. As for the other parts of the palace, they seemed to be equally beautiful. The walls were inlaid with gold and shone with such radiance that it seemed the house created its own daylight, even when the sun did not shine. Every room and doorway was filled with light. The furniture was as magnificent as the house, and the palace could easily be taken for Jupiter's residence on earth.

Drawn by such loveliness, Psyche timidly approached the doorway, and then, gathering confidence, she stepped over the threshold. The hallway lured her in, and she walked from room to room, admiring everything she saw, until she came to a storeroom filled with treasures. But what amazed her more than the countless treasures was that nowhere did she see a bolt or bar or guardian. As she was gazing about in pleasure, a voice suddenly spoke, as if responding to her thoughts. "My lady, why do you marvel? All that you see is yours. But you must be tired. Why not go to your bedroom and rest? And when you wish, a bath will be ready. We, your voices, are here to attend to your comfort, and afterwards, to serve you a banquet fit for a queen."

Psyche was grateful to whatever divine will was watching over her and protecting her. She followed the advice of the voice, and her fatigue soon slipped away with sleep and a refreshing bath. Psyche then noticed a semicircular table that was set for dinner with a comfortable couch in front of it. Happily, she stretched out on it, and immediately food and wine were set before her. She saw no human, yet she heard voices, so she understood that the voices were the servants. After she had eaten, an invisible being sang. Then another played the harp. A chorus of beautifully blended voices ended the evening's pleasures.

With the coming of dusk, Psyche went back to her bedroom. As night approached, a pleasant sound came closer. It was the steps of her bridegroom.

At that moment, Psyche began to shiver and tremble, for she was afraid for her maidenhood. She feared what she did not know. As she trembled, her unknown bridegroom slipped into her bed and made her his wife.

Before dawn, he disappeared. Soon after he left, the voices entered her bedroom and reassured and comforted the young bride about the loss of her virginity. Her bridegroom came the next night and the next. And what began as a strange custom soon became a great pleasure. And so Psyche's life went on. At night, her bridegroom visited her, and in the day, the voices were her company.

Meanwhile, her parents were growing old with their constant grief and weeping. News of Psyche's sad fate and their parents' grief reached the two sisters, and they left their homes to console their parents.

That night, Psyche's husband, whom she only knew from touch and hearing, warned her, "My sweet Psyche, my dear wife, fortune is cruel, and a terrible danger threatens you that you must be prepared to meet. Your two sisters, disturbed by the account of your death, have returned to look for you. They will soon go to the rock from which Zephyrus carried you. If by chance you hear their cries, you must not answer, or even look up, for if you do, you will bring great sorrow to me and utter ruin to yourself."

Psyche agreed. She promised she would do as her husband wished, but when he and the night had disappeared, she wept all the next day. She felt herself a prisoner in this beautiful palace, deprived of human conversation, unable to comfort her dear sisters or even to look at them. All that day she did not eat or bathe or enjoy any entertainment. That night her husband came to bed earlier than usual. Taking her in his arms, he said, "Is this what you promised me? What shall I expect from you next? You have cried all day and all evening, and even as I hold you in my arms you continue to weep. Very well, do as you wish. Follow your destructive desires. Unfortunately, you will remember my warnings when it will be too late to repent."

Psyche entreated her husband. She threatened to take her life. She had to see her sisters, to comfort them, to speak with them. At last, he consented to his bride's wishes and even agreed to give her sisters gold and jewels. But he warned her over and over, to the point of frightening her, "Do not let your sisters persuade you to try to find out my identity. If you do, you will fall from the height of your good fortune and out of my arms forever."

"Oh no, no!" she cried. "I'd rather die a hundred times than be without your sweet lovemaking. I do not know who you are, but I love you. I love you desperately. I love you as I love my own soul. I would not give you up for Eros himself; but please, grant me one more wish, and command your servant, the West Wind, to carry my sisters to me as gently as he carried me to you." Psyche pressed her persuading lips on his. She murmured sweet sounds and wrapped her arms and legs more tightly around his, whispering, "My sweet husband, you are Psyche's own soul." Coaxed by her caressing words, her husband felt his will drown under the force of her kisses. Then, at the approach of dawn, he disappeared.

After several inquiries, the sisters were informed of the place where Psyche had been abandoned. They climbed the mountain, and when they reached the rock, they wept so loudly that the cliffs echoed with their wretched cries, *"Psy-che! Psy-che!"* The sounds of their grief reached Psyche in the valley below, and she ran from the palace and cried, "Sisters, stop your wailing! Do not torment yourselves for no reason. The one for whom you mourn is alive. Dry your eyes and you will soon embrace her." Psyche then alerted Zephyrus to her husband's commands, and he took a gentle breath and lightly carried the sisters to the valley.

When the three sisters saw each other there was a flurry of embraces and frenzied kisses. Once again they burst into tears, but this time their tears were tears of joy. Then Psyche said, "Come into our house, dear sisters, come inside and restore your tired spirits." Psyche showed them the luxuries of her golden palace and introduced them to the voices. "Bath!" she called.

And a bath was soon ready. "Food! Wine!" And a splendid dinner was laid on the table. The sisters ate and drank and looked about the palace, and a great envy arose in each of them. Then one of them began to press Psyche with questions. "Sister, how did your husband come by such riches? Who is your husband? What does he look like? How does he treat you?"

Remembering her promise to her husband and not wanting to reveal their secret, Psyche invented, "Oh, he's . . . very handsome, he's . . . a hunter with a soft, downy beard, and . . . and . . . he wanders over the hills and countryside—"

"A hunter!" both sisters exclaimed. "A hunter with a palace like *this?*"

Sensing their disbelief, Psyche was afraid that she might reveal more than she wanted, so she quickly went to the treasure chest and drew out necklaces and bracelets. She filled her sisters' laps with jewels and summoned the West Wind to carry her sisters back to the mountain.

When the sisters arrived at the rock, they were in such a fury that they began to speak in the same moment. The older one said, "How stupid and cruel and unjust fortune has been to us! Is it fair that three sisters should be given such different fates? You and I, who are the oldest, are banished from our homelands and married to foreign husbands who treat us like slaves, while she, who is the result of our mother's last weak effort at child-bearing, is given riches beyond measure and a god for a husband. Why, she doesn't even know how to make use of such riches!"

"Sister, did you see what was in that palace? Dresses, jewels, gold—gold! Even the floor was set with gold. And if her husband is as handsome as she says, why, no woman on earth can be as happy as she. What's more, if his affection for her continues to grow, this godlike husband of hers might make her a goddess! She already acts as if she were one, ordering about her voices, commanding the wind. As for me, my husband is older than

Father, balder than a pumpkin, as puny as a boy, and locks up every chest in the house with bolts and chains!"

"Oh sister, what about *me?*" cried the younger. "My husband is so doubled over with backaches, he hardly ever gets into my bed. I'm not a wife. I'm a nursemaid. I spend my time ungnarling his twisted fingers and ruining my hands with putrid compresses."

"No, sister, you are too patient, too servile in the way you accept your situation. I will speak freely, for I believe in saying what I think. I cannot bear the good fortune of our sister. Nor can I bear how arrogantly she behaved toward us, boasting and bragging as she showed us around and then throwing us a few trinkets when she tired of us and ordering the wind to sweep us away. No! I am not a woman drawing this very breath if I do not topple her from her great height. And if you are equally insulted, as you well should be, then let us work together to find a sure plan. We must not tell our parents or anyone else about what she has given us. Nor should we tell anyone about her being alive or her riches. It is enough that we know. If we do not tell anyone that she is rich, she will not be rich. A person is only rich when others know about it. She will soon find out that we are not her servants but her older sisters. Now, let us go back to our husbands and homes, and when we can think of a plan to humble her, we will meet again."

The wicked sisters agreed. They hid the treasure Psyche had given them. They tore their hair. They mangled their miserable faces with grief. They let their eyes run with false tears and brought even more distress to their parents. Then they hurried to their homes, their minds scheming with thoughts to bring about the destruction of their innocent sister.

Meanwhile, Psyche's unknown husband again warned her, "Oh Psyche, do you not see the danger that awaits you? A perilous storm will soon be here and if you do not prepare for it, it will carry you away. Those treacherous little she-wolves are plotting your destruction. They will urge you to see my face, but as I have warned you, if you were to see it, you would lose me forever. If these hateful witches come to see you, as I know they will, you must not speak to them; and if you cannot do this because of your open and simple nature, then at least, you must not listen to or answer any of their questions about me. This is most important, for soon we will have our own family. In your young womb, a child is growing. If you keep our secret, the child will be born a god. But if you betray our secret, the child will be born a mortal."

Psyche was delighted at the thought of bearing a divine child and thrilled with such an honor. She happily repeated to herself the joyful name "mother." She counted the days as they came in and the months as they went by, and since she was innocent, she marveled that the loss of her maidenhood should cause her belly to swell to such a size.

But now those revolting furies, breathing out serpentine slime, were again traveling to the palace. Once more, Psyche's husband warned her, "Today is the last day. Those of your own sex and blood have taken up arms against you. They have broken camp, drawn the battle-line, and sounded the bugle. Their swords are sharpened and pointed at your throat. A great disaster hovers near you. Have pity on yourself and on me. Keep our secret safe and protect us from the misfortune which threatens to ruin us. Refuse to listen to those wicked women who, with the hatred they bear you, do not deserve the name sister. Do not listen to their sirenlike cries that will cause the rocks to echo with their false lamentations."

Psyche burst into sobs and said, "Do you not trust me? Did I not prove my loyalty to you last time? I did not give away our secret before, nor will I do so tomorrow. I beg you, command the West Wind to perform his duty as he did last time, as my consolation for not seeing you. I implore you, by your sweet curls, by your wonderful smell of cinnamon, by your soft, smooth cheeks, by your warm chest and face—which I shall know by the face of our child—grant me my wish. Let your Psyche, who is devoted to you, be happy, and I will not try to see your face or be afraid of the dark shadows again. I will be content to be in your arms, for you are my light." Enchanted by her words and soft kisses, he wiped away her tears with his hair. He promised to grant her wishes and departed before dawn.

Driven on by their carefully composed plans, the two sisters did not stop to see their parents but went directly to the rock. Without waiting for the West Wind, they rashly leapt from the summit. Zephyrus, although unwilling, obeyed his master's commands and arrived, panting, just in time to catch the sisters and carry them safely to the valley below. Immediately they rushed into the house, crying, "Sister, sister!" and embraced their victim. Then, covering their treacherous desires with smiles, they fawned and said, "Oh Psyche, you are no longer a slim girl but a mother. What a joy for all our family! How delightful it will be for us to take care of your golden child. If he matches his parents in beauty, as he surely will, a new little Eros will be born!"

Taken in by their seeming affection, Psyche called for the delights of the palace to be prepared. "Bath! Food! Harp! Flutes! Chorus!" Although they saw no one, the sisters enjoyed these sweet serenades, yet the honey-sweet softness of the songs did nothing to change their bitter plans for revenge. The sisters soon guided the conversation to their own ends.

"Psyche," one said, "tell us about your husband."

"Yes," the other said, "we want to know every detail. What kind of man is he? Where was he born? Who is his family?"

Poor, simple Psyche. She had forgotten what she'd told them last time, so again she invented, "Well, he's . . . a merchant from the next province. He's very rich . . . middle-aged . . . has gray in his hair—" Suddenly, she stopped abruptly and hurried to the treasure chest. She loaded presents into the arms of her sisters and had them carried away.

As the West Wind ferried them, they began to debate in midair. One said, "Sister, have you ever heard such outrageous lies? One minute her husband is a young man with a beard, the next minute he has white in his hair. Who is this man who dances so quickly into old age? Either she's lying, or she's never seen her husband. Whichever it is, we must remove her riches from her as quickly as possible."

"But sister," the other said, "if she has never seen her husband, it may be that she is married to a god and the child she is bearing will be divine. If that is so, and she has slept with a god and is to become the mother of a god, I shall hang myself from the paneled ceiling! In the meantime, let us go to our parents and return in the morning with our plans firmly set in our minds."

In a state of nerves, they spoke to their parents scornfully. They could not sleep all night but tossed and turned because of their fury. As soon as morning came, they rushed to the rock and, by means of their usual escort, impetuously descended to the meadow. By pressing on their eyelids they were able to force out a few tears. Then they spoke to Psyche and said, "Oh sister, you live in a state of bliss, for you are ignorant of the danger that threatens you. But we, who have made inquiries concerning your affairs, are in anguish about what we have discovered, and we can no longer conceal it from you: A huge, bloodthirsty snake with many coils, whose gluttony knows no bounds, secretly finds his pleasure with you at night. Oh Psyche, remember the Oracle of Apollo that foretold that you would wed a cruel, fierce beast! Hunters and neighbors living nearby have reported seeing him returning in the evening from the pasture and writhing his way toward the palace. They say he is indulging you, fattening you, until the time is ripe and your womb is full; then he will devour both you and the child. Make up your mind, it is your choice. You can return to safety with us or be buried in the entrails of a savage beast. But even if you choose to live here with your wild voices and indulge in secret bestial couplings, at least we, your sisters, have done our duty."

Poor, simple Psyche. When she heard her sisters' ghastly disclosure, she turned stiff with horror. The blood went out of her face. She gasped. She forgot all her husband's warnings and all her promises. Stuttering and faltering, she breathlessly said, "Oh yes, yes, dear sisters, it is right that you have persisted in your duty. In fact, I am afraid that those who told you such things have not lied. You see, I have never seen the face of my husband, nor do I know where he comes from. He speaks to me only at night and flees my bed before dawn. Perhaps he is this dreadful beast that you describe, for whenever he comes to me at night, he insists that I must not try to see his face; and when I have questioned him, he has threatened me with dire warnings. It's very painful to me that he's so afraid of the light. Yes, surely he is some kind of monster! Oh sisters, what shall I do? Please! Advise me, otherwise all your care and kindness will have been in vain."

Once the wicked women had opened the gates to Psyche's soul and seen her defenses fall away, they pressed their advantage and openly assaulted her frightened spirit. One of them said, "Because you are our own flesh and blood, it is our duty to forget all danger for your sake. After careful reflection, we have thought of a plan, a plan which you must follow exactly, for it is the only one that will lead to your safety. This is the plan: Sharpen a knife and hide it under the side of the bed where you usually sleep. Then, get an oil lamp and hide it behind a curtain near your bed. After the beast has climbed into your bed and is sleeping soundly, slip out of your bed. On tiptoe, get the lamp from its hiding place. You will be able to carry out your heroic deed with the help of its light. Take the knife in your right hand, then strike with all your force and cut off the poisonous snake's head at its neck. We will be waiting nearby, and when we hear your signal we will help you gather the treasures from this palace. Then we will find a true man for you, not a beast."

When they saw that their words had inflamed the heart of their sister and she was ready to carry out the deed, they fled. They were terrified to be near, should such a disaster occur. The West Wind carried them to the rock, and they hastened to their ships and sailed away as quickly as they could.

Psyche was left alone, except for her rages which tormented her. All day her mind tossed back and forth like the waves of the sea. At first she was clear and determined, but soon she began to waver, distracted by the implications of what she was about to do. She delayed. She hurried. She dared. She feared. She despaired. She raged. And what was most curious was that in the same moment, in the same body, she hated the beast and she loved the husband.

As night approached, she made her decision and prepared the necessary equipment. In the darkness, her husband slipped into her bed, and they wrapped themselves in the combats of love. Then he fell into a deep sleep. By nature, Psyche did not possess a particularly bold spirit or body, yet the cruelty of her fate hardened her. She took the lamp and seized the knife. But the moment the light shone on the bed, the mystery was revealed: Lying on the bed, in all his beauty, was the sweetest and gentlest of all creatures, Eros, the God of Love. At the sight of him, the light of the lamp burned more brightly and the knife dulled its edge in shame.

Psyche was terrified. Pale and shaking, she fell to her knees. She tried to hide the knife by plunging it into her own heart, but the knife, fearful of such a crime, fell from her hands onto the floor. Then, despite her weakness and fear, her spirit revived when she gazed at Eros' divine beauty. His golden hair was still wet with nectar. His playful curls drifted across his rosy cheeks and milky white neck. They glowed with such splendor that the light of the lamp flickered in awe. On his shoulders the flying god's dewy white wings sparkled with beauty, and although they were not in flight, the outermost feathers reverberated in continuous quivering. The rest of his body was so smooth and splendid that Venus herself would not have been ashamed to have brought such a child into the world. At the foot of the bed lay the weapons of the great god: his bow, quiver, and arrows.

Psyche's insatiable curiosity impelled her to examine and touch each of her husband's weapons. She took an arrow from his quiver and, wishing to test its sharpness, pressed her thumb against it. Because her hand was trembling, she pierced her skin, and several drops of blood ran from her finger. So it was that by her own will, yet unknowingly, Psyche fell in love with the God of Love. Burning with desire, she leaned over and kissed him impulsively, impetuously, with kiss after kiss after kiss, fearful he would waken before she had finished.

While the anguished and delighted Psyche hovered over him, the lamp she was holding, whether from treachery or jealousy or simply from desire to touch and kiss such a body, spurted a drop of boiling oil onto the right shoulder of the god. Oh rash, bold lamp! Oh paltry minister of love, how could you burn the God of Fire, you who were surely invented by some lover who wished to behold the sight of his beloved past the moment of darkness?

Eros awoke and leapt out of bed in dreadful pain. When he saw his wife holding the lamp in her hand and the knife lying on the floor, he understood. Without a word, he spread his wings and flew into the air. Psyche caught hold of his right leg and held fast. With her weight dragging him, they flew into the cloudy regions. She held on until her strength gave out. Then she let go and fell to the ground, exhausted.

Eros did not desert her as she lay on the ground. He flew to the nearest cypress tree and, swaying from its top branches, reproached her. "Oh most simple Psyche, why didn't you trust me? Rather than obey the commands of my mother, Venus, who ordered me to cause you to love and be bound in marriage to a wretched, worthless man, I flew from heaven to love you myself. Yes, I acted rashly. I, the famous archer, wounded myself with my own weapon so that my wife might take me for a monster and try to cut off my head with a knife—my head and eyes which once bore you so much love. Oh Psyche, did I not try to warn you? Did I not plead with you to listen to me? Well, your other advisors will soon pay their penalty. As for you, you will be punished by my flight." With these words, he flew away.

Psyche lay on the ground and let out dreadful cries as she watched her husband fly farther and farther away. When she could no longer see him, she sprang up and threw herself into the river to end her life, but the waters of the river, fearful of the God of Love, who can even burn waters, would not let her die. They lifted her up and carried her to the other shore.

There, by chance, Pan, the shepherd god, was sitting on a flowering bank. He was caressing the mountain goddess, Echo, and teaching her to repeat soft notes on a reed pipe. Nearby, a flock of she-goats frolicked, feeding on the grass. Pan called softly to the girl, saying, "My dear child, although I am a countryman and a shepherd, I have not lived all these years without learning a sign or two. Some may call it divination; I say it is simply keeping one's eyes open. By your wavering step, your paleness, your tear-stained cheeks, your incessant sighs, and your sad eyes, I would suppose that you are desperately in love. Listen to me. Do not try to take your life by leaping from a cliff or in any other way. Put aside your grief and go to the great God of Love. Although he is a spoiled, whimsical creature, you can woo him if you speak to him softly and gently and offer him your services and prayers." So the shepherd god spoke. But Psyche could not reply. All she could do was to bow and go on her way.

Psyche wandered and did not know where she was going. Toward evening, she arrived at the city where the husband of one of her sisters was king. She asked to be announced to her sister, who received her at once. After they had exchanged embraces, the sister asked her the cause of her visit. Psyche said to her, "Do you remember the advice you gave me? You told me I should strike with a knife the miserable beast I slept with before he could devour me. Well, I followed your advice. But when I shone the light on my husband, I saw the most heavenly sight: It was Venus' son, Eros, who was sleeping quietly in my bed. At the sight of such a great god, I was both overjoyed and horrified, and while I stood there confused, the worst accident happened. Several drops of boiling oil spurted from the lamp and burned his shoulder. He awoke from his sleep in terrible pain, and when he saw me with the lamp and knife, he cursed me, saying, 'If that is your intention, go! Go from my bed and take your things. I will marry your sister' (and he said your name); 'I will marry her in a proper wedding ceremony.' Then he ordered Zephyrus to carry me far from his palace."

The sister could hardly wait for Psyche to finish speaking. Filled with raging lust and jealousy, she ran to her husband, made up some lie about the death of her parents, and quickly set sail. At the rock, although the wind was blowing in the opposite direction, she cried out, "Eros, take me. I am yours. Take me, for I deserve it! Zephyrus, carry down your new mistress!" Then, with a great leap, she threw herself toward the valley. But not even her corpse found a resting place. As she deserved, her body was smashed to pieces by the rocks and crags, and her entrails were scattered across the cliff, providing a feast for vultures and wild animals.

The punishment of the next one was not long delayed. Psyche's wanderings led her to the palace of her other sister. With the same story, she deceived this sister, who also eager to replace Psyche, rushed to the rock and called out, "Eros, take me, I am yours!" Then she leapt from the rock and was met by the same fate.

Psyche continued her wanderings. She wandered through many lands searching for Eros, not knowing that he was lying in his mother's bedroom, groaning in pain.

A white bird, a kind of gull that skims over the waves, plunged into the waters to speak to Venus, who was bathing in the sea, as she often did to renew her virginity. The bird twittered, "What a scandal! Your son is severely wounded and lies moaning in your golden bed. Gossip is spreading and the insults to your family name are mounting. Because both of you are gone, he to his mountain harlot and you to your seaside holiday, pleasure, grace, and elegance have disappeared from the earth, while rudeness and vulgarity reign supreme. There is no longer any concern for marriage, friendship, or children. All relationships are in disorder, and if anyone makes a commitment to another person, he is regarded as acting in very poor taste."

Before the meddlesome bird could go on, Venus, who was troubled by the abuse of her son's reputation, interrupted and asked, "Has my beardless, naive boy finally taken a mistress? Well, you seem to be the only one who has remained loyal to me. Tell me, then, who is she? A nymph? a grace? An hour? One of the muses?"

The bird needed little prompting. "No, my lady, not a nymph or a grace or an hour or a muse, but a human! He has fallen desperately in love with some girl, and if I remember her name correctly, it is Psyche."

"Psyche!" Venus shrieked. "My rival! Has he chosen to love

my supplanter? If so, then I have become his procuress!" Rising from the sea, Venus continued to rage as she returned to her golden room, where she found her son in bed, as the gull had reported.

From the doorway she spoke in the loudest voice she could command, "What kind of son are you? Is this behavior of yours appropriate to your birth and name? First you trample the orders of your mother, as if I were not your parent, and then, instead of tormenting my enemy with a horrific love, you court her with puerile embraces, turning my enemy into my daughter-in-law! Trifler! Panderer! Do you imagine that you can do as you wish because you are my only child and I am too old to have another? Well, not only can I have a more worthy child than you, but I shall adopt the son of one of my servants and give him your wings and torch and bow and arrows, all your playthings, which were not given to you for the purpose for which you have used them.

"You were improperly raised by your father! From your childhood, you've struck your elders, even your mother, shaming me by piercing me almost daily with your arrows. You show no fear of your brave, warlike stepfather, but incite my jealousy by happily toasting the young women he falls in love with. You shall soon repent of your sport and pay bitterly for this marriage!"

Then Venus spoke to herself, musing, "Now that I have been insulted, where shall I go? How shall I restrain this little lizard? Shall I ask help from my enemy, Sobriety, whom I have so often offended with my wanton ways? What horror, to have to converse with that unsophisticated bore! But Vengeance is a great comfort. Yes, she is the one, and none other, whom I must summon. She will castigate my trifler, unstring his bow, take away his arrows and quiver, extinguish his torch, and restrain his body with other bitter remedies. When she has shaved off his golden locks that I myself so elegantly arranged, and clipped his lovely wings that I dyed from the milk of my breast, then I shall be appeased!"

Venus stormed out of the palace full of bitterness and met the two great goddesses, Ceres, the Goddess of the Harvest, and Juno, the Goddess of Marriage. When they saw Venus' fierce expression, they asked her what had happened to dim the charm of her shining eyes.

"I am glad you are here," Venus answered. "You have come in time to ease the rage in my heart. I want you to help me to find that fugitive Psyche, for I am certain that you are not ignorant of my son's unspeakable deeds."

"Yes, yes," said the goddesses, who knew well what Venus was referring to and wanted to soothe her wrath. "But what horrendous deed has he committed that you want to condemn his pleasure and to destroy the girl he loves? Is it a crime to court a pretty girl? Have you forgotten how old he is? Or that he is a man? Perhaps you think of him as a boy because he is still so charming? As a mother, and a woman of the world, why do you want to spy on him and repress those excesses, those very inclinations, that you yourself delight in? How can you incite desire in all hearts while you forbid its presence in your own home?"

The goddesses defended Eros in this way because, although he was absent, they too feared his arrows. But Venus, enraged that her injuries were treated so lightly, turned from them abruptly and hastened toward the sea.

Meanwhile, Psyche wandered day and night seeking her husband. She hoped to appease his anger either by gentle words of love and flattery or by servile pleas for forgiveness. She saw a temple high on a wooded hill and thought, "How do I know this is not my husband's dwelling? Eagerly, yet painfully, she climbed to the top of the mountain. Upon reaching the summit, she went directly to the shrine and saw corn sheaves, barley, and harvest implements which had been abandoned by the farm laborers because of the heat and were scattered over the floor in disarray. Psyche carefully arranged everything in its proper place, hoping to gain the protection of whatever deity the temple belonged to.

As she was diligently working, Ceres, whose temple it was, noticed her from a distance and called to her. "Psyche! Poor Psyche. Venus is in a rage and is searching for you everywhere. With all the strength of her powers she is seeking revenge. Why, then, are you looking after my affairs instead of concerning yourself with your own safety?"

Psyche threw herself at the goddess' feet. Her hair streamed out on the floor. Her tears moistened the goddess' sandals. She pleaded with her, begging for protection. "Great, holy goddess, I implore you, by the cornstalks in your hands, by your joyful harvest festivals, by the secrets in your baskets, by the winged chariots of your servant dragons, by the furrows of the Sicilian earth from which the chariot wheels of Pluto arose and carried off your daughter under the earth to a dark marriage, by Proserpine's torchlit return, and by the other secrets concealed at Eleusis and your Athenian temples, help your suppliant! Let me hide just a few days under the sheaths of corn in your temple until the anger of Venus has subsided. I am so tired. Give me a moment of quiet to regain my strength."

Ceres said, "Your tears and prayers touch me, and I wish I could help you, but I cannot go against my relatives, and I have been friends with Venus for years. You had better leave quickly and be glad I have not held you as prisoner. Now go!"

Not expecting to have her hopes so quickly disappointed, Psyche started down the mountain more miserable than before. As she walked, she saw in a valley another temple glimmering in a dark grove of trees. She went toward the temple, not wanting to overlook any deity who might offer her protection. She saw luxurious garments hanging on the branches of the trees and the doorposts of the temple with the name Juno embroidered on them. They were offerings to the goddess for the favors she had granted.

Psyche knelt before the altar. Wiping away her tears, she held the warm altar and prayed, "O sister and wife of the great god, Jupiter. If you are in Samos, whose ancient shrines exult in your birth and infancy, or in Carthage, where you are worshiped as the virgin who drives across the heavens in her lion chariot, or in Argos, presiding over your renowned walls near the bank of Inachus, where you are celebrated as the wife of the Thunderer and the Queen of the Goddesses, wherever you may be—you are worshiped in the east as Zygia, the Goddess of Marriage, and in the west as Lucina, the Goddess of Childbirth—for me, you are Juno the Deliverer and can free me from my burdens. May you be Juno the Protectress for me and care for me and my child, for we have wandered all these days and all these nights. They say you protect women such as I who are with child and in great danger."

Juno then appeared in her grandeur and majesty to Psyche and said, "I wish I could favor your prayers, but it would not be proper for me to go against the will of Venus. She is my daughter-in-law, and I love her as my own daughter. Besides, I am forbidden by law to give refuge to a fugitive without the owner's consent."

This second turning of fortune against her so terrified Psyche that she gave up her search for Eros and abandoned any hope for her own safety. Where can I find protection? she thought. Where can I find refuge, if even the goddesses, although they are willing, can not help me? In which direction can I go that a trap is not waiting for me? Under what roof, in which shadow, can I hide from the inescapable eyes of the great goddess?

As she walked, she felt her destiny in her feet and said, "Psyche, you must take courage. Seize your own manly spirit. There is no escape. Although it may be too late, go to Venus and humbly beg her forgiveness. Perhaps in her house you will find your husband."

So Psyche prepared to submit to her fate, even if it meant her death. Carefully, she considered in her mind the first words she would say when she met Venus.

Meanwhile, Venus had given up seeking vengeance on earth and decided to appeal to the heavens. She ordered her chariot to be prepared. Her husband, Vulcan, had painstakingly carved this chariot from tiny gold filings and had presented it to Venus before their honeymoon. Four white doves willingly came forward and offered their rainbow-colored necks to be harnessed to the jeweled yoke. Sparrows followed the chariot playing and chirping, announcing Venus' arrival. The clouds parted. The heavens opened with joy at Venus' appearance, and little singing birds showed no fear of either the eagles or the rapacious hawks.

Venus drove directly to Jupiter's palace where she formally asked permission to use the services of the great messenger, Mercury, for her purposes. Jupiter nodded his azure blue brow in consent, and Mercury joined Venus in her chariot. As they descended from the heavens, she anxiously implored her Arcadian brother, "Dear brother, as you know, I have never undertaken anything of great importance without your help. Surely you must have heard that I have been searching for a long time for my lost fugitive. I need your assistance. I want you to make an announcement in every town that a reward will be given to anyone who finds her. You must describe her clearly and exactly in every public place so that no one will be able to offer the excuse of harboring her out of ignorance." Venus then presented Mercury with a long résumé, which began with Psyche's name and continued with all pertinent details. Having done this, she returned home.

Mercury obediently flew from country to country and made his announcement: "Hear ye! Hear ye! If anyone can seize in flight or reveal the hiding place of Venus' fugitive servant, whose name is Psyche, let that informant look for Mercury at Venus' sacred mountain. There he will receive seven kisses from Venus and, more than that, one sweet thrust from her honeyed tongue." At the thought of such a reward, great rivalry and desire were immediately incited in the hearts of all men. The news also ended Psyche's wavering.

Psyche was about to enter the gates of Venus' palace when one of Venus' servants, whose name is Custom, recognized her and cried loudly, as loudly as possible, "You wicked wretch! At last you acknowledge that you have a mistress! Or do you pretend to be ignorant of how much trouble we have had in searching for you? I am glad you've fallen into my hands, and no one else's, for here you will be troubled no more with earthly disease. Now that you are in hell you will pay for your arrogance." Custom seized Psyche by the hair and dragged her into the palace. Psyche struggled in vain.

When Venus saw who was being led into the palace, she let out an hysterical laugh, the kind that often bursts out from angry people. She scratched behind her right ear, where the Nemesis of each person lies. Then she shouted, "So, you have deigned to visit your mother-in-law? Or perhaps you have come to inflict further wounds on your husband whose life is already endangered? Oh do not worry, I will receive you as is proper. I will receive you as the good daughter-in-law that you are. Grief and Anxiety, where are you, dear servants?" When they appeared, Venus said, "Take our visitor and treat her properly." They led Psyche away, and following their mistress' commands, they whipped and flogged her, torturing her in the most extreme ways. Then they brought her back to Venus.

Once again, Venus laughed harshly and cried, "Did you think you would get my pity because of your big belly? From this belly you would give us an illustrious offspring, turning me into a happy grandmother. Grandmother? At my age, shall I be delighted to be called a grandmother and have the son of this disgusting slave called my grandson? Nonsense! Although my son enjoys his games, marriage is not permitted between a god and a mortal. Moreover, there were no witnesses, and the father of the bride did not give his consent. Therefore, even if we allow you to survive and to give birth, the child will be a bastard."

Then Venus pounced on Psyche. She tore her clothes. She pulled her hair. She shook her. She shook her back and forth violently, striking her again and again. "Ugly, broken harlot!" she shouted at her. "Where is your beauty now? Who will love you now? Do you have any merit, any diligence, any endurance left? Well, we shall test your worth!"

Then she took great quantities of barley, millet, poppy, chick-peas, and beans and threw them in a great heap on the floor. "Separate this pile," she said, "so that each seed is in its proper place by evening, at which time I will return to inspect your work." Giving the pile a quick kick, Venus left to attend a wedding feast.

Psyche did not even stretch out her hand toward the pile of seeds but sat there overcome, stupefied, silent. Then an ant, a tiny tiller of the field, appeared. He saw the enormity of the task and took pity on the wife of the great god, for he hated the cruelty of the mother-in-law. Running energetically to and fro, he summoned an army of neighboring ants, calling to them, "Nimble ones, children of Mother Earth, the wife of the great God of Love is in danger. Come quickly! Let us help her."

Wave after wave from this six-legged nation came forward and speedily placed all the grains in their proper piles. Then they disappeared.

At nightfall, flushed with wine and smelling of balsam, Venus returned from the feast wreathed in gleaming roses. When she saw the perseverance that had gone into completing such a task, she said, "Not you, harlot! No, this task was not done by your hands, but by someone whom you lured into your service. Well, you shall both suffer for this." She threw Psyche a coarse crust of bread and went to her room. In another room in the same house, Eros was shut up, in part so he would not injure himself further, and in part so he could not meet his beloved. For the lovers, separated and yet together under one roof, the bitter night slowly passed.

As Dawn rode in, Venus called to Psyche and said, "Do you see the grove on the other side of the river? Sheep graze there whose shining fleece is the color of gold. Bring me their precious wool, however you can."

Psyche set out willingly. She did not intend to follow Venus' commands but rather to throw herself from the cliffs into the river and put an end to her sufferings. Yet as she came near the river, a soft breeze blew, and a green reed whispered to her, "Psyche, I know what sufferings you have endured, but do not pollute my waters with your death. Wait. If you cross the river at this hour when the sun is in its full strength, the sheep, who have terrible tempers, will turn in fierce madness against you. They will gore you with their horns and attack you with their poisonous teeth. But if you wait until the heat of the day is past and the sheep are resting, lulled by the coolness of the afternoon breeze, then you can cross the river and hide behind the tall plane tree which drinks from the river, as I do. As soon as the sheep have stopped their fitful grazing and are calmly resting, you can gather their golden fleece, which you will find clinging to every bush and branch in the grove." Through the kindly reed's advice, Psyche easily accomplished her theft and brought Venus back an armful of golden fleece.

But Venus offered Psyche no warm response to the successful completion of her second task. Instead, she narrowed her eyebrows and, smiling bitterly, said, "I am not deceived. The secret author of this deed does not escape me. Your own prudence and courage will be tested with the next task. Do you see the summit of that great mountain over there? Dark waves of water run from its peak into the River Styx. Take this crystal jar and fill it with those icy waters. Then return to me immediately." As she handed Psyche the jar she repeated her hideous threats.

Psyche hurried away, eager to end her miserable life. When she reached the first hill, she saw the impossibility of the task that was demanded of her. From a huge, inaccessible boulder, black waters gushed out of a cave and poured into a narrow hole that led into a channel which flowed directly into the earth. On either side of the hollow cave, two fierce, long-necked dragons with never-closing eyes guarded the waters. The waters themselves spoke in their own protection, hissing, "Depart! What do you wish? Beware! Take care! Away! Death!" Psyche knew that there was no possibility that she could accomplish such a task. Not even the consolation that comes from tears was hers. She could not weep. She turned as still as stone. Her senses left her. Only her body remained.

Her grief did not escape the eye of kind providence. Remembering his debt to Eros, who had brought Ganymede to heaven to become his cupbearer, Jupiter sent his royal bird to earth. With widespread wings, the great eagle flew to the wife of the God of Love and said, "Simple girl, how do you hope to steal or even touch a single drop of that awesome water? All the gods, even Jupiter, are terrified of the Stygian waters. As you mortals swear by the name of the gods you fear, the gods swear by the waters of the River Styx. Here, give me that jar."

He grasped the jar, and with quickly beating wings, dodged zigzag between the dragons' rows of savage teeth and three-forked quivering tongues until he arrived at the waters. But the waters would not give themselves up to him until he lied to them and told them that he had come at Venus' command. He filled the jar and gave it to Psyche, who gratefully accepted it and quickly returned to Venus.

Even then, the wrath of the offended goddess was not appeased. She became more menacing. She smiled at Psyche cruelly and threatened her with a further task, saying, "You have carried out my tasks so easily because you are a sorceress and a witch. But I have one more service to ask of you: Take this box, my puppet," and she gave her Proserpine's box. "Carry it yourself to Pluto's dreaded dwelling. Give Proserpine the box and say, 'Venus asks you to fill this box with a little of your beauty, not very much, just enough for one day. Unfortunately, she has used up her supply while caring for her sick son.' Then return quickly, for I need it to dress tonight before I go to the theater of the gods."

Psyche knew that her end had come. The veil was lifted. She was being sent to her death. Who could deny it? She was being asked to travel, on her own feet, to the shades, to the lowest part of Tartarus. Well, the fastest, easiest way to reach hell was to climb the highest tower in town and jump to her death. But when Psyche arrived at the tower, she heard it speak and say, "Foolish one, why do you want to destroy yourself? Why do you collapse before this, your final task? If your spirit is separated from your body, you will go to the depths of Tartarus, but you will not return.

"Listen to me. Go to Taenarus, a well-known city in Lacedaemon. It is not far from here. It borders on the desolate places. There you will find a hole, a breathing place for the god of the underworld. Go through this opening. It will be dark and pathless. Trust yourself. It will lead to Tartarus. But do not go empty-handed. In each hand, carry a honey-barley cake, and in your mouth carry two coins.

"After you have traveled through the darkness a long way, you will meet a lame driver and a lame donkey carrying wood.

The driver will ask you to give him some twigs that have fallen from his load, but you must not help him or answer. Pass by quickly. When you come to the River Styx, Charon, the ferryman, will ask to be paid. For a fee, he takes travelers on his boat to the far shore. Greed is everywhere, even among the dead. Neither Charon nor his great father, Pluto, will do anything without being paid. A poor man who dies needs travel money, and if by chance he does not have a coin in his hand, he will not be allowed to die. Give this disgusting old man one of the coins you are carrying, but let him take the coin with his own hand. While you are crossing the sluggish river, a corpse, which is floating on the surface, will raise his rotting hands and beg you to take him into the boat, but I warn you, pity is not permitted, show him no pity.

"Once you have crossed the river, you will see three old women who are weaving. They will beg you to help them. You must not touch their material. It is a trick, a trick from Venus who wants you to let go of one of the barley cakes. This would be no small loss, for if you lose one, just one, it will be fatal. Without the second barley cake, you will not see the light of day again.

"After you pass these women, you will see a huge dog with three horrid heads whose barking terrifies the dead, although he can not harm them. He never sleeps. He sits at Proserpine's dark door and guards the empty house of Pluto. Throw him one of your barley cakes and you can enter easily. Then you will meet Proserpine, who will receive you graciously. She will invite you to sit on pillows and will offer you fine food and drink. Sit on the ground and ask only for coarse bread. Then tell her why you have come, and she will give you what you want.

"On your way home, give the raging dog the other barley cake and the greedy boatman the coin you have saved. Once you have crossed the river, you will see the dance of the constellations again. But one thing, one thing I must warn you above all, do not, do not open or look into the box which you will carry or be too curious about the hidden treasure of the divine beauty."

And so the far-seeing tower advised Psyche, through prophecy, how she might complete her task. With a barley cake in each hand and two coins in her mouth, Psyche set out for Taenarus. She entered the breathing hole leading to the dark regions. Silently, she passed the lame driver and donkey. She paid the ferryman, ignored the floating corpse, spurned the three weavers, appeased the horrid dog's rage with a honey-barley cake, and entered the palace of Proserpine. She refused the soft cushion and tasty delicacies. She sat humbly on the floor and ate coarse bread. On Venus' behalf she announced her errand. Proserpine secretly filled Venus' box and gave it back to Psyche sealed. Psyche tricked the barking dog's rage with the second barley cake, gave the remaining coin to the ferryman, and returned from the underworld.

Once she was on earth again and had given thanks for the glorious light of day, although she was eager to complete her last task, she was suddenly seized by an overwhelming curiosity. "Would I not be a foolish woman," she said to herself, "to hold in my hands a box of divine beauty and not use the smallest amount to make myself more beautiful for my own lover?"

She lifted the cover of the box. No divine beauty awaited her. Instead, a deathlike Stygian vapor poured over Psyche, enveloping her in a dense cloud of sleep. Psyche sank to the ground and lay there like a corpse.

At that moment, Eros, whose wound had been healed, could no longer bear to be separated from Psyche. He flew through the highest window in the bedroom where he had been imprisoned. His wings, strengthened from their long rest, carried him swiftly to Psyche. He carefully wiped the cloud of sleep from her body and returned it to the box. Then, with a harmless prick of his arrow, he woke Psyche and said, "My love, again you almost perished because of your curiosity. But now take my mother the box, and I will see to the rest." With these words Eros flew away, and Psyche immediately brought Proserpine's gift to Venus.

Utterly consumed with his passion, but fearing his mother's stern reproach, Eros fortified himself from the wine jar. Then he spread his wings and crossed the great expanse of heaven to plead his case before Jupiter. Jupiter stroked Eros' cheeks and kissed his hand and said, "My son and master, you have never treated me with the respect which is due to my position. Instead, whenever you have wanted to, you have shot your arrows into my heart, where the law and order of the universe lies. You have disgraced me on frequent occasions with earthly lust, which is contrary to Julian law and public order. You have injured my reputation with sordid love affairs transforming my divine beauty into serpents, flames, wild beasts, birds, or bulls. Nevertheless, I will be moderate, for I remember nursing you on my knees. I will grant your request, but at the same time, I warn you: Do not forget those gods who can be envious because of the beauty of your wife, and take care that you find for those gods a similarly beautiful woman. And bring her to me as quickly as possible."

Jupiter then ordered Mercury to announce to all the gods and goddesses that they were to appear in the theater that night and if they were absent, there would be a fine of 10,000 drachmas. This small warning allowed the theater to be completely filled. After the roll was called and the names of the gods and goddesses were read from the Book of Muses, Jupiter spoke. "All of you are familiar with this rascal, Eros. I need not inform you of his daily indiscretions and adulteries. But the time has come for his raging passions to be restrained and his wildness fettered with the knot of wedlock. He has chosen a girl and made her his wife. Let him now keep this girl, Psyche. Let him cherish her and delight in her, now and always."

Then Jupiter turned to Venus and said, "My daughter, do not worry that your lineage or rank will be lessened because of a marriage to a mortal. I will arrange theirs to be a marriage of equals and join them together according to civil law."

He then ordered Mercury to bring Psyche up to heaven. When she entered the theater, Jupiter held up a goblet of ambrosia to Psyche and said, "Drink, Psyche, and you shall become immortal. Eros will not leave your embrace, and for you both, your marriage will be eternal."

A sumptuous wedding feast began. Jupiter embraced Juno, and the other gods and goddesses did the same. Ganymede, Jupiter's rustic cupbearer, poured Jupiter a cup of nectar. Bacchus served the others. Vulcan prepared the meal. The hours made all things glow with roses. The graces scattered blossoms about the hall. Apollo took up his lyre and played so well that Venus danced with great delight. Then the satyrs and Pan joined in on their pipes.

So it was that Psyche married Eros. And when her time came, she bore a child, a little girl, and they named her Joy.

LAYLA AND MAJNUN

"Let me Love for Love's Sake!"

For Marie-France Racine

Long ago in the desert of Arabia there lived many great chieftains. The greatest of the chieftains was the chieftain of the tribe of the Banu Amir. He had wealth beyond imagining: piles of gold and jewels, precious silks and carpets, herds of the finest goats and camels. But rich as he was in worldy goods, he was richer still in the goodness of his heart.

He ruled with perfect justice. He was generous. He welcomed every traveler to his camp. His tribesmen prospered. They loved and honored him. And the sayyid, as this chieftain was reverently called, was content, but for one thing: he had no heir.

As the years passed, the sayyid became more discontented. He did not consider all that fortune had given to him, but instead, he brooded on what he had been denied. "Of what use are my jewels and gold, if I have no one to give them to? A man does not live if he has no son to carry on his memory." He prayed. He increased the fervor of his prayers, and, at last, God gave him his heart's desire: His wife gave birth to a son.

At birth, the infant Qays was of extraordinary beauty. When he was two weeks old, his face was as round and beaming as the full moon, and every year his beauty increased. During this time the sayyid was known to have said, "Is there any man on earth as fortunate as I?"

When the boy was of school age he was sent to study. He was so quick of mind that when he was given a pen, he mastered writing, and when he was given a book, he learned to read. He excelled in all disciplines, but most of all, he excelled in the art of conversation. His schoolmates delighted in listening to him, for when he spoke, his words were as sweet as music, his wit as sharp as an arrow, and his wisdom as lustrous as a pearl.

Then one day, after several years, the daughter of a mighty chieftain came to study in the school. This little girl was like a jewel that one seldom sees. She was as slender as a cypress. Her skin was as white as milk, her lips and cheeks the color of roses, and her dark eyes, both gentle and bold, could pierce a man with one glance. Because of her lustrous black hair, she was called Layla, which means night.

From the moment Layla entered the classroom, Qays could neither read nor write. He could only stare at her in wonder. "Layla . . ." he whispered, as if in prayer, "Layla . . ." All that day and all the next, he could say no word but Layla.

As the days passed, while the others played in the courtyard or studied, Qays did nothing but gaze at Layla. Soon the other children noticed what was plain to see, and since they were too young to understand love, they laughed at Qays. They pointed at him and said, "Qays has lost his heart! Qays has lost his head! Qays loves Layla!"

Qays tried to hide his love, but his eyes returned of their own will to Layla's face. As for Layla, she would lower her head and blush. Then she would raise her head, blush and smile shyly back at Qays. Each of them had become intoxicated with the scent of a flower which has no name. At night they went eagerly to their beds to dream of each other. And in the morning they rushed to school so they could inhale the fragrance of their love.

But the other children missed Qays. They were jealous of his affections for Layla. Behind the teacher's back they taunted him: "Have you heard? Qays loves Layla! Qays loves Layla!"

At last, Qays could no longer contain himself, and one day, in the middle of the classroom while the others were reciting their lessons, he stood up and shouted, *"Layla! Layla! LAYLA!"* Then he ran from the classroom into the streets and bazaars shouting her name, "Layla! *LAYLA!*" People who watched him shook their heads and said, "He is a *majnun,* a *majnun.*" And so it was that Qays came to be called Majnun, which means madman.

When Layla's father heard that a young man had insulted his tribe by shouting his daughter's name in the streets, he ordered Layla to be taken from the school and brought to the desert camp where she was confined to a tent.

Majnun sat listlessly in the classroom staring at her empty place. When he could no longer bear her absence, he fled to the desert and walked until he came to the tribe of Layla's people. He hid behind a tree and waited, hoping for a glimpse of his beloved.

One night, Layla, restless and sleepless, went to the door of her tent. Majnun suddenly appeared, and in the moonlight, they gazed at each other. They saw reflected in each other's faces their own fear and pain and love. Neither stirred or spoke a word. When dawn came, Majnun turned and fled.

After that evening Majnun lost his heart. And as he lost his heart, he lost his reason. He wandered in the desert, and as he wandered, he tore his clothes and wildly sang his songs. From afar, people would say, "There goes Majnun, once called Qays. Because of his love of Layla, he wanders in the desert and brings dishonor to his father and his tribe."

The chieftain of the Banu Amir grieved greatly. He summoned his counselors to him, and each gave an account of what he had heard. After careful consideration, the chieftain said, "My son has lost his senses. Layla is the jewel through which he sees the world. If he wins Layla, his senses may be restored."

So the chieftain set out with a small delegation of counselors and a caravan of camels laden with precious gifts. The sayyid was received with friendliness and deference by Layla's people. After feasting, the sayyid said, "I have come to ask for your daughter's hand in marriage. My son wishes to drink from your daughter's pure fountain. I am not ashamed of such a request. I have wealth and followers and can be a great friend or a formidable enemy. State your daughter's dowry, and I will pay. Be wise, for tomorrow the price may fall."

But Layla's father was a proud man. "Do you imagine that you can change fate by wishing?" he said. "You speak of the outside, but what about the inside? All the world knows of your son's madness. Shall I mate a flawless gem with a faulty one? No! Cure your son first, then you may mention marriage."

Sadly, the sayyid returned to his camp and told his child what Layla's father had said. "Love's fool," he said to his son, "why must you worship only Layla? In our tribe there are a hundred sweetly scented girls, with lips like hyacinths, who are as lovely as the springtime. They are surely as beautiful as Layla. Be patient and you will have what you want. The sea consists of tiny drops of water, the deserts of tiny grains of sand. Bliss will come. It is the turquoise in the seal of God. Let your happiness grow slowly. With patience you will find another stone—even more precious. I tell you, forget Layla; choose another. Then you will be happy."

Majnun cried out in despair. Why did his father not understand? It was Layla—only Layla—that he loved.

He fled again to the desert. He tore his hair and sang songs of Layla. He wandered from village to village. At first crowds of villagers followed, jeering him, but when they came closer and heard his words, not one who listened failed to weep for the singer and his fate.

But Majnun did not see or hear them. He had fallen into emptiness. It was as if his name had been torn from the Book of Life. He cried to Layla, "My beloved, send a greeting, a message, a word. I know you are in prison, but I am starving for a token, a gesture from you. I have given away everything. My only companion is my shadow, but I do not speak to him, for I do not wish you to have a rival. Once I had your shadow, but that, too, has been taken from me. Now what is left to me? What hope? My love for you is a riddle which has no solution; it is a code that cannot be deciphered."

He wandered aimlessly until his strength gave out. Then he fell down and prayed for death. "Let the rocks fall and crush me. I am an outcast. I bring shame to my father and my tribe. Let me be freed from myself and my shame."

From a nearby hill, a group of shepherds saw Majnun fall. They came and made a litter for Majnun and carried him back to the camp of the Banu Amir. There he lay in his own tent, singing songs and calling Layla's name.

With a heavy heart the chieftain called his counselors again and said, "Does not the whole world go to Mecca to ask God's blessings? Let us too pray to the Almighty One to cure Majnun."

And so in the last month of the year, the month of the pilgrimage, the sayyid and his kinsmen departed from their camp and traveled to Mecca. They devised a litter for Majnun, and Majnun was carried as gently as if he were an infant in his cradle. When they entered Mecca, the sayyid showered gold coins on the crowds of people. Then, trembling with hope, he brought Majnun to the shrine and taking his hand, said softly, "My son, ask God to save you from your passion. Pray to him to end your madness. Pray to him that you will be cured."

Majnun pulled his hand away and laughed wildly. Then he stretched his hands to the shrine. He touched the stone and cried, "Oh God, let me not be cured of love, but let my passion grow! Let me love for love's sake! Take what is left of my life and give it to Layla. Make my love a hundred times greater than it is today!"

When the sayyid heard Majnun's prayers, he bowed his head in grief. The caravan returned to the camp of the Banu Amir. "I have tried," the sayyid told his kinsmen, "but Majnun will never be cured. Before the holy shrine he blessed Layla and cursed himself."

News of Majnun's laughter at the holy stone soon spread throughout Arabia. When Layla's father heard, he was incensed. "This madman destroys the honor of our tribe. He wanders in the desert dancing and kissing the earth. The people gather about him and listen and learn his songs. My daughter's name is on every man's tongue." Layla's father sent two emissaries to the sultan's court to register his complaint.

"Majnun is a man possessed," the messengers said. "He dishonors our tribe. Order him to be punished so that the name of Layla will be unstained."

"So be it. Let him be punished as you wish," the sultan's prefect said. When a kinsmen of the Banu Amir, who was at the court, heard the sultan's words, he hastened to his tribe to inform the sayyid.

At once the sayyid, with his tribesmen, set out to find Majnun. They searched the desert and after many days found him in a desolate gorge. He was moaning and sighing, talking in verse. His body was wasted, his bones were showing through his skin.

When Majnun saw his father, he wept. "Haven of my soul, forgive me, Father. Forgive me. What can I do? I am not the one who holds the thread of my fate."

"My son, you are young. Youth has led you into confusion.

Each of us has a weakness which we hide from the world. Our true friends reveal our faults so we can cure ourselves. I am your friend. Let me be your mirror. If you would marry, you must learn to control yourself. You must learn patience and prudence.

"Layla's father will seek you with the sword. You mean more to me than life itself. Do not abandon me. Return to your tribe so you may be protected, and those who love you may bring you laughter and happiness."

"My father, your majesty is as great as heaven itself. I kneel before you. Your words scorch me, but I cannot change my destiny. All creatures are ruled by destiny. To love Layla is my fate. I cannot throw off my burden. And why should I be afraid? He who goes in search of his beloved is not afraid. My soul is in the fire. No man can harm me."

The sayyid brought Majnun from the rocky gorge to his tent. His kinswomen brought him food and water, and his mother whispered soothing words. His childhood friends came to entertain him, but to Majnun they were all strangers. He stared blankly in the cool darkness of the tent. Even his mother was a stranger to him. After three days, he tore open the curtain of his tent and fled again to the wilderness. He roamed the desolate country of rocks and sand. His feet became like iron. The people mocked him. They jeered him, and yet, they could find no fault with his songs.

In all this time, Layla had become more beautiful. Her gazelle's eyes caught every man who chanced to gaze at her; her midnight tresses bound them to her. She was thought to be the most beautiful girl in all of Arabia. On the outside she blossomed, but on the inside she was devoured with sorrow. From morning to night she burned for Majnun. She did not reveal her love to anyone but repeated his name through the hours to her shadow. She lived between fire and water—the fire of her passion and the water of her tears.

And yet, her lover's voice came to her, for he was a poet and no tent could keep out his verses. Every child in the bazaar knew his songs, every wanderer in the desert repeated his poems.

Layla heard his songs and secretly composed her own. She wrote them on scraps of paper and threw them to the wind. Any passerby who found Layla's songs knew for whom they were intended and brought them to Majnun, hoping for a reward of a song. Thus the wind carried the lovers' melodies to and fro across the desert.

Not far from Layla's tent was a palm grove which Layla and her companions often visited. One afternoon the girls were singing and laughing and playing. Layla withdrew from the others to sit under a tree and speak with her grief. "My faithful one, if only the garden gate would open and you would walk in. You would sit next to me and we would gaze into each other's eyes. You are like an elm tree and I . . . But perhaps, you have already suffered too much for my sake?"

At that moment, she heard a voice cry from outside the garden wall, "Oh Layla, how can your heart be so frivolous, while mine is wounded by the arrows of the night?"

When Layla realized it was Majnun's voice, she burst into tears and wept bitterly. One of her friends went to Layla's mother and told her that Layla's heart was still devoted to Majnun. Layla's mother began to watch Layla. She saw her steal out of the tent at night and stand by the gate, waiting. She saw her toss tiny notes to the wind. But she was afraid to speak to her daughter. She was afraid of her daughter's grief. She was silent. Layla was silent. And both grieved.

Some days later a young man from the tribe of Assad who was journeying across the desert caught a glimpse through the wall of Layla sitting in the palm grove with her companions. The man, whose name was Ibni Salam, was from a rich and noble family. He was nicknamed Bakht, because he always had his way in all his desires. As soon as he returned home, he sent a matchmaker to Layla's father with a generous offer. Layla's father was pleased with the offer, but he said, "Be patient and wait. My daughter is delicate. Give the bud time to ripen." Ibni Salam had no choice but to wait.

During this time Majnun continued to sing his songs and wander through the desert dressed in rags and crying out Layla's name. One day a Bedouin prince named Nowfal passed the gorge where Majnun lived and saw a long-haired, naked creature crouching by a rock. At first the prince did not know whether what he saw was human, animal, or demon. When he heard the creature weeping, he said, "Who is that woeful being?"

"That is Majnun," he was told. "He has left his tribe to live in the desert. Day and night he composes love songs for his beloved. People come to visit him and bring him food and drink. But he hardly eats. He drinks very little. He lives only for Layla, his beloved."

When the prince heard this, he wanted to help the devoted lover win his heart's desire. He ordered his men to set up a tent in front of the cave and to prepare all kinds of delicacies. But Majnun refused the food and would not respond to any of Nowfal's entreaties. Nowfal was about to give up hope when he spoke Layla's name.

At the sound of Layla's name, Majnun looked up as if he had been touched by the morning sun. He smiled at Nowfal and repeated, "Layla . . . Layla . . ." Soon he began to sing, and as Majnun sang, Nowfal listened in amazement and thought, This creature is no madman, he is a great poet.

"You shall have your Layla," Nowfal said, "even if I must

fight for her myself. I promise you: Layla will be your wife."

Majnun leapt up and embraced Nowfal. His face glowed with happiness. But a moment later, he became fearful and cried, "But how? Her parents will never agree. They will say, 'Shall we give a flower to the wind?' No, others have tried before. Do not deceive me with false promises."

Nowfal was even more taken with Majnun's passion and replied, "Do you doubt me? I swear to you, I swear to you in Allah's name, by his prophet Mohammed, that I will fight for you like a wolf—no, like a lion. I will fight until Layla is yours. But, in return, you must show some patience. Tame your wild heart, if only for a few days."

Majnun went with the prince to his camp. The prince gave Majnun fine robes and a silk turban. In the prince's company, Majnun became the cheerful young man he had once been. In the mornings the prince and Majnun rode in the desert. In the evenings they feasted, drank wine, and listened to the songs of the minstrels. Majnun's bent and wasted figure uncurled and he began to walk again like a tall reed swaying in the sun. Nowfal was delighted by the change and daily offered his new companion precious gifts. After a week, he became so attached to Majnun that he would not leave his side even for an hour.

But the days Nowfal spoke of turned into months, and one afternoon as they were sitting together, a shadow passed over Majnun's face and he said, "My friend, how can it be that you do not feel my grief? I can not wait any longer. I beg you, keep your promise. Let a thirsty man drink!"

Majnun looked so mournful that Nowfal leapt to his feet and took his sword. He rallied a hundred of his devoted followers and set out for Layla's camp. When he arrived at the camp, Nowfal sent a herald with this message: "I, Nowfal, have come with an army prepared to defeat you. Bring Layla to me so she may be given to the man who is worthy of her. Let his longing be satisfied. Otherwise, we will destroy you like an all-devouring fire."

The herald returned with this reply from Layla's father: "Do you intend to steal the sun? The decision is not yours. I will not give my daughter to a madman. Draw your sword; we know how to break you."

Nowfal then sent a stronger threat and the chieftain replied with further curses. Nowfal was boiling with rage. He set out toward Layla's tribe, which by then had prepared for battle. When the two armies met, a great crash was heard in the desert as if two mountains had been hurled against each other. Swords and spears ripped apart breasts and limbs. Blood from the wounds of the warriors poured into the sand.

But Majnun did not take part in the fighting. He watched the battle and trembled. He trembled not from fear but from suffering. He suffered for both sides. Each blow was a torment to him whether it struck a friend or an enemy.

As the battle continued, Majnun became more confused. He was willing to die for Layla but he had never intended to have those Layla loved killed. Each time one of Layla's people was struck, Majnun wept. At last he entered the middle of the battle and cried to God for peace.

One of Nowfal's warriors, seeing Majnun standing in the battlefield praying, cried to him, "This is not the moment for noble tears. Take up your sword and fight the enemy. Have you forgotten that we are risking our lives for you?"

"But who am I to fight?" Majnun said. "Your enemies are my friends. If my beloved's heart beats for your enemy, then I must defend the enemy. My home is my beloved's heart. I wish to die for my beloved, not to kill men."

Nowfal fought unflinchingly, but when the sun set, Majnun turned on Nowfal accusingly and said, "Your promises were great but what have you done? You have destroyed any possibility for me to be united with Layla. Now she must hate me for the harm done to her family."

"What could I do?" Nowfal protested. "The enemy outnumbered us both in men and arms. But I promise you I will not rest until Layla is yours."

Nowfal sent messengers to all the tribes from Medina to Baghdad. He opened his treasure chests and assembled an army that stretched, like an ocean of iron, from horizon to horizon.

Several days later, at dawn, he attacked again. Layla's tribesmen fought bravely. Nowfal fought in the front line, cutting a man's life with each stroke of his sword. The sand turned red. There was so much blood and destruction that by afternoon, even the swords were afraid to strike. Before night, victory belonged to Nowfal.

As a sign of defeat, the elders of Layla's tribe sprinkled earth on their heads. They knelt before Nowfal and kissed the ground. They said, "You are our victor. Before you, we place our swords and spears. We beg you to allow those of us who remain to go in peace."

Nowfal was glad to be finished with such grief. "Bring me the bride," he said. "Then you and your tribesmen may go in peace."

An old man stepped out of the crowd of defeated tribesmen. He knelt humbly before Nowfal. He bowed his forehead to the dust. He was Layla's father. He said, "I am old and broken and disgraced by all the blood that has been shed for me. You are my master. But I do not accept that my daughter be given to a madman. Before I will allow her to be given to a man who has disgraced his name and hers, before I would eat at his table, I will kill her with my own hands."

Nowfal was moved by the chieftain's fervor. Tears came to his eyes. Then one of Nowfal's advisors spoke. "The old man is right. Majnun is not fit or stable. When we fought for him, did he not pray for peace? Did he not roam the battlefield, blessing our enemy and weeping with sorrow when our enemy died? He laughs and cries without reason. Such a man cannot be trusted."

Seeing that the defeated chieftain was adamant and that his men had turned against Majnun, Nowfal gave orders to break camp. As they rode from Layla's camp, Majnun angrily accused Nowfal, "Faithless friend, why did you do it? Why did you let my hopes ripen and then let them drop in despair? Was it for your own glory? Oh faithless friend, did you ever intend to let me have my treasure?"

Without waiting for an answer, Majnun cried out, *"Layla! Layla!"* and turned his horse and galloped off into the desert. Nowfal searched for Majnun, but he did not find him that day, or the next, or ever again.

Majnun rode many days without stopping. He passed abandoned campsites. He spoke to himself of his faithless friend. He had no companion but the desert wind.

One day he saw in the distance three small black figures. He rode closer and saw a hunter about to kill two gazelles he had captured. When Majnun looked at the gentle eyes of the gazelles he thought of Layla's soft black eyes and cried, "I beg you, do not harm the animals. Have they hurt you? Creatures such as these are not meant to be burned. I am your guest so you must heed my wishes."

The hunter had never heard anyone speak like this. "But what am I to do?" he said. "I want to obey you but this is the first catch I have made in two months. I have a wife and children to support. If I spare the animals, my family will starve."

Without hesitating, Majnun jumped from his horse and placed the horse's reins in the hunter's hands. Happy with the exchange, the hunter rode away. Majnun kissed the eyes of the gazelles and freed them.

Then Majnun walked. The sand scorched his feet, thorns ripped his clothes, but he did not notice. At night he crawled into a cave for shelter.

The next day toward evening, he came upon another hunter who had caught a stag in his snare and was about to kill it.

"I beg you," Majnun cried, "release the poor creature. Let it live. If his mate had words, what would the hind say tonight without her companion? Imagine her suffering! Imagine yours—if you were caught in the trap and the stag were free."

"The animal is mine," the hunter said. "I do not need to kill it, but I need to survive. If you wish, I am willing to sell it to you."

Majnun opened his bag and laid at the hunter's feet what remained of the possessions that Nowfal had given him. The hunter was pleased. He accepted Majnun's offering and went away.

Majnun went up to the stag. He caressed him gently, saying, "Are you, like me, far from your beloved?" He removed the cord binding the stag's feet. "Be off!" he said. "Flee! Search for her. Rest in her shadow. That is your place. And should you pass the tent of my beloved, tell Layla that though I am far from her, she is always with me. Tell her that no animal moves or bird sings that does not bring her memory to me. Tell her, tell her, my friend."

Majnun watched the stag gallop off across the sand. It was now night. The stars came out. Majnun covered his eyes and wept. When he awoke, he wanted to be near Layla. He began to hurry toward her camp, but after a time his strength gave out and he fell to the ground in a daze.

In the morning he opened his eyes and saw two strange figures approaching. An old woman was dragging an old man by a rope.

The old man's arms and legs were bound with chains. The man was shouting as if he were out of his senses.

"Stop!" Majnun cried to the woman. "Who is this man? And why are you torturing him? What has he done?"

"He is innocent," the woman said. "He is a dervish and I am a widow. We both have no house or food or way to live. We travel this way so that people will think he is mad and take pity on him and give us food or charity. Whatever we are given we divide between us."

Majnun fell on his knees and said, "Release him. I am the one who is mad. Tie me up, put chains on my legs, and take me with you. You can keep for yourselves what I am given."

The woman agreed. She freed the dervish and put the chains around Majnun. When they came to a village or even a shepherd's hut, Majnun would sing his songs. Despite his chains, he would dance like a drunkard. He would beat his head on the stones. The woman would hit him, and they would be given scraps of food.

So they wandered until one day they came to an oasis and Majnun recognized the tents of Layla's people. He hit his head against a rock. Tears poured out of his eyes. "Layla! Layla!" he cried. "Oh Layla, look at me. Because I made you and your people suffer, I am doing penance. I have given up my freedom. I stand before you chained. You are my judge. I am your prisoner. I am guilty even when I am innocent. Stroke my hair, cut off my head, do as you wish with me. I am as trusting before you as Ishmael was before Abraham, and yet, I do not dare to see you."

Then, with a great howl, Majnun tore off his chains. He flung them away and ran from Layla's tents and from the old woman toward the mountains.

Soon after Majnun had fled to the mountains, Ibni Salam returned to claim his bride. He brought caravans laden with gifts of gold and silver for the chieftain. He was an eloquent and noble man as well as a mighty warrior. His honor and name preceded him. He brought protection and force. His words could melt a stone. Thousands of men obeyed him. Layla's father did not refuse him.

The wedding feast was set. Carpets were spread. For seven days and seven nights the wedding was celebrated. There was food, laughter, and gaiety. The guests admired the bride's wedding presents, and no one, not even the women, suspected the despair in Layla's heart.

After the wedding festivities, Ibni Salam left at dawn with his bride. When the caravan reached the lands of the tribe of Assad, Ibni Salam stretched his arms from horizon to horizon and said joyfully, "My beloved, everything you see is yours. My possessions are yours. My kingdom is yours."

But that evening Layla refused to go to his bed. The next night, she refused. And the next. For a time, Ibni Salam was gentle. But Layla still refused. Then, out of desperation, he tried to force her. Layla struck him and said, "If you touch me again, I will take my life. You may force me, but I have sworn by Allah that I will never submit to you."

Ibni Salam loved Layla so deeply that he agreed to her wishes. He even asked her forgiveness. "I would rather be permitted to look at your face than to lose you forever." So it was that Ibni Salam longed for Layla. Layla longed for Majnun. And a year passed.

During that year Majnun wandered in the wilderness. One evening he was lying under a blossoming thorn tree singing Layla's name when a stranger approached stealthily, like a snake. He stopped a short distance from Majnun and rasped in a voice of a demon, "Idolator! Fool! You sing to your beloved, but she is lying in the arms of another man—her husband. Do you think she refuses him? No! She thinks only of kissing and lovemaking and pleasures. She is like all the other women—fickle and faithless. Never trust a woman. She is peace on the outside and turmoil within. The man who believes in a woman's fidelity is even more stupid than the woman who causes him to suffer."

The man heard a thud and a moan. Majnun's head struck a stone so hard that blood spurted onto the earth. The rider's heart was suddenly caught and spun around.

"Listen to me," the unknown man cried. "I was lying, wickedly lying. Layla has not deceived or betrayed you. She was forced to marry, but she has never gone to her husband's bed. She has remained faithful to you."

Then the stranger heard Majnun begin to weep. Majnun wept, not knowing which of the words the stranger had spoken were true. The stranger rode away.

At the camp of the Banu Amir, Majnun's father was growing weak with age. He was not afraid of death but he did not want to die without seeing his son. He set out with two men from his tribe and asked every stranger for news of his son. At last he came upon a Bedouin who said, "Majnun? The mad singer? He is in a cave in the desert, but you will not find the cave. It is too far and too desolate."

The old sayyid insisted. He crossed vast plains, lonely mountains, oceans of sand. Often he thought he would never find his son. But then he asked himself why he had lived, if not for his son? Of what point was all his wealth, if there was no one to give it to?

At last he came to the cave and saw a man hardly more than a skeleton who moved on four legs like an animal. Could this ghostly, serpentine creature be his son? Overcome by love and sorrow, the sayyid went to the ghostly figure and tenderly caressed his head. Majnun looked up. He saw a man weeping but did not know who he was. "Who are you?" Majnun asked. "What do you want?"

The old man said, "I am your father."

When Majnun heard his father's voice, he cried out. Then he put his head in his father's lap and wept uncontrollably. Father and son wept and kissed each other and held each other.

After a time the sayyid spoke and said, "It is enough, Majnun. You must overcome your grief or it will devour you. Think of something else. Tempt yourself. Why not? Enjoy the moment. Do not trust in tomorrow. Act as if your life is in death's hands. A woman wears only what she has woven. A man reaps only what he has sown. Even if life has not kept its promises, life is still before you. Majnun, my son, I beg you, come home with me. I am close to death, and I want to spend my last days with you."

Majnun listened to his father. He put on his silk robe and the turban his father had brought. For some days he ate and drank with his father and did not sing to his beloved. But when the time came for them to return, Majnun said, "Father, I want to obey you. But I cannot. I am no longer the same man. I am a stranger to my tribe. If you asked me how this happened, I do not know. I know you are my father, and I know that I am your child. But I do not remember your name."

The sayyid listened to Majnun and realized that Majnun no longer belonged to him. Then he took Majnun in his arms and said, "Majnun, you are my yoke and my crown. Hold me fast, my son, for this hour must nourish me for all time. Hold me so I may have wonderful dreams in the cradle that is being prepared for me. Soul of your father, we shall not see each other again in this lifetime."

Two days after the sayyid returned to his camp, he died. He

chose the moment of his death and so his fate. His soul fluttered to rest before the throne of God.

One evening a kinsman from the tribe of the Banu Amir who was hunting in the desert came upon Majnun and told him that his father had died. Majnun went to his father's grave and prayed and wept and begged for forgiveness.

"Oh father," he said, weeping, "You were so gentle and I was so hard. A thousand times you offered your hand and I refused you. You prepared banquets and beds for me and I refused. You could not rescue me, but you shared my suffering. You were my companion, my protector, my pillar. Now that you are gone, I have no home, for my home was in the corner of your heart. Oh father, I have shamed you, forgive me."

As he made his way back into the desert, he came upon a group of Arabs who stared at him. A paper fluttered from their camp and landed near Majnun's feet. He picked it up. It said two words: Layla—Majnun. It was written in admiration of their devotion.

Majnun tore it in half. And then he tore up one of the names.

The people watched in surprise. One person dared to ask him why he had destroyed one of the names.

"With lovers," Majnun answered, "only one name is needed."

"But which name did you destroy?"

"Layla's."

"Layla's?"

"Do you not understand? The name is only the veil. Layla is the face under the veil."

When Majnun returned to his cave, the animals of the desert came to live with him. First the lion, then the stag he had saved, the antelope, the wolf, the fox, the wild ass, the hare, the timid gazelles. In time, even the vulture came to live with them. No animal ever harmed another. In Majnun's presence the animals had no fear of each other. Majnun was king and his cave was his court. All around were rocks and thorns and burning sand. No place on earth was more desolate, yet Majnun called it paradise because he lived in peace with his friends.

Every day Majnun and his animals wandered in the desert and dug among the stones for roots and herbs. As the sun set, they feasted together. Majnun spoke of Layla and sang his songs. The animals listened quietly and bowed their heads. When darkness fell, the fox with his bushy tail swept clean Majnun's resting place, and Majnun lay down to sleep. Throughout the night until dawn, the lion and the wolf kept watch.

Once as Majnun gazed fondly at his animals, he thought, I who live among my friends am surely the happiest man of all, and he told them the story of the king of Merv and the courtier. . . .

"Once there was a young courtier at the palace of the king of Merv. The king kept a pack of ferocious dogs and whenever he lost his temper, because someone had displeased him, he had that person thrown to the dogs.

"The young courtier who heard the victims' cries and the dogs' barking decided he would become friends with the dogs. First he spoke with the keeper of the dogs. Then he brought the dogs food. In time when he appeared the dogs would wag their tails and he was able to pat them without danger.

"One day, for no apparent reason, the king lost his temper and ordered the courtier to be killed. The guards tied his hands and feet and threw him into the kennels. But when he was given to the dogs, they were glad to see their friend and licked his face and hands and wagged their tails.

"That evening, the king missed the courtier and regretted his order. He asked about the boy and was told that the boy was most likely an angel, for the dogs would not harm him. The king went to see this miracle boy. The ferocious dogs were nestled happily about him. The boy was released.

"Several days later, the king sent for the boy. He took the boy aside and said, 'Tell me the truth. I do not believe in miracles. How did you stay alive?'

"The boy was too clever to lie. 'Your Majesty,' he said, 'for six years I served you faithfully. But in one moment you forgot my existence. The dogs whom I befriended for six months were grateful to me because of the few chunks of meat that I fed them.'

"The boy spoke with daring. The king freed the dogs and tamed the wild beast in his own soul."

One night Majnun awoke. The night was as light as day. The sky was a resplendent garden of flowers. The planets, holding human fate, danced between the stars. Majnun looked from planet to planet, wondering which one might help him. When his glance fell on Venus, he called to her, "Mistress of dancers and singers, you light up the sky for all who seek happiness. Your hand holds success, your wine sparkles in every goblet, your gift brings life to the tongue. Be gracious to me, too. My soul is sick. Who but you can heal it? I beg you, let me breathe my beloved's scent before I die."

Then he called to the great planet, Jupiter, "Star of delight, the structure of the world is yours. You give my fate grandeur. My heart draws its strength from you. You are the one who cares for the souls, who determines our fates. Help me! Help me—if there is help for me."

The planets continued on their way. They were governed by another ruler. Majnun cried in despair. The planets were silent. The stars were silent. Then he cried a third time. He cried to the ruler of the stars and planets and said, "You who created the earth, whose name is the wellspring of all names. The seven heavens lie at your feet. Venus and Jupiter are your servants. All things great and small obey you. I was earth, heavy and soiled. You have changed me to water. Do not let me perish now. Do not let me lose my way."

After Majnun had prayed, a deep calm came to him. His eyes closed. He slept and he dreamt of a tree rising from the earth. From one of the branches, a bird flew toward him; from its beak, a drop of light, like a jewel, fell on his head.

When Majnun awoke in the morning, he was flooded with a feeling of happiness that he had not felt in many years. That day an old man with a flowing white beard approached Majnun's cave. The animals growled, warning Majnun. But Majnun quieted them.

"Grandfather," Majnun said, "I do not know you, but I like your face. Still, I do not wish to be bitten again by a stranger. If you come with painful words, retrace your steps."

The stranger fell before Majnun and said, "Noble creature, you have made the wild animals your companions. I am not your enemy but a friend who carries a message from your beloved. A secret message. But if you prefer, I will leave."

Majnun's heart began to dance and he cried, "No! Speak! Speak quickly!"

"A few days ago I passed a tented camp. Nearby was a grove of palm trees and a garden. Through the palm trees I saw a light, as if the moon had just risen behind one of the trees. When I looked closer, I saw it was not a planet or a star but a young woman whose beauty surrounded her like light. She was a shining goblet reflecting the secrets of the world. But her head was bent in sorrow and she was weeping. I approached and asked her, 'Who are you? And why are you weeping?'

"She answered, 'Do you want to wound me even more? Stranger, once I was Layla; now I do not know who I am. Majnun is thought to be mad, but I am madder than he is. He is at least free to wander where he wishes. But I, I have no one to talk to, no one to trust. I swallow dry grass so as not to speak the poison in my heart. Night and day I burn. Love cries to me, "Flee!" Reason admonishes me, "You are not a falcon; you are a partridge." Love cries, "Flee!" Reason shouts, "You are not a man; you are a woman. Beware of disgrace!" But tell me, stranger, do you know of Majnun? Speak to me of him. How does he spend his days? Where does he stay? Who are his companions?'

"I told her what I knew of you, for who does not know of you? 'Majnun is without family or friends.' I said. 'His only companions are the wild animals of the desert. Suffering has broken him. His father has died. He writes of grief and love.' Then I told her some of your lines which I know by heart.

"She sighed and trembled and wept. She sat so forlorn lamenting your father's death and your memory that I thought she would die. Then suddenly she made a decision and asked me to bring you a letter."

The old man took a letter from his bag. He kissed it and gave it to Majnun. Majnun stood there as if he were dreaming. He stared at the letter. Then, as if a demon possessed him, he tore off his clothes and began to dance—faster and faster, wilder and wilder. He leapt into the air and whirled around and around until he fell to the ground motionless. Yet his fingers still gripped the letter. When he returned to his senses, his first glance was at the letter. He broke the seal and read:

"I begin my letter to you in the name of the king who gives life to the soul. Wiser than all men, the king understands the language of those who cannot speak.

"As a prisoner, I write to you. I know you have broken your chains. I do not know where you live, but every dawn and dusk I see your blood on the mountains. The others slander you, but I know you have remained loyal to me, and I, to you. True, I have a husband. He has fame and dignity but who he is means little to me.

"I heard of your father's death and beat my face as if my own father had died. Do you understand how I wish to share your grief?

"The rock splits and crumbles but the jewel that is enclosed is untouched. My diamond is intact.

"I am yours."

Like a starving man, Majnun devoured every word of her letter. For a long time he could only say, "Oh God." Then at last, he asked the old man for a pen and paper and sat down and wrote to Layla, scarcely pausing, for the words he needed had been ripening all this time in his heart.

Majnun wrote:

"In the name of the one who has made the heavens and causes the sap to rise in the springtime, who knows the rock and the precious stone hidden within the rock, who knows the hidden chambers of the human heart, listen to my prayer—

"My garden of paradise, you say I am the keeper of the treasure-house. But I do not have the key which opens the gate. I am a tree in your forest. But you have changed my day to night, stolen my heart, seduced me with words and made a bond with another man.

"My ruby, when will this tie with your husband be broken? Even if your husband is a noble man, why should a stranger be permitted to enjoy your beauty? He is a thief who has been given that which he has not paid for. When will the door to the treasure-house open? When will you let me in?

"It is not that I suspect you or that I hate your husband but rather that I long for you. I long for your breasts as sweet as jasmine. But even if your faith is hidden from me, you lead me on the path, revealing the true nature of love. It does not matter if there is no salve for my wound. You teach me to forget myself.

You caress me and engrave my name in a sheet of ice which melts daily in the sun."

Soon after the messenger left with Majnun's letter, another visitor approached Majnun's cave. He was Salim Amiri, the brother of Majnun's mother. He was wise and noble and reputed to be able to find a way out of every impasse. He loved Majnun dearly and often sent gifts to him through caravans, wishing to ease his nephew's misery. He hoped that this might be the moment to bring Majnun home.

"Who are you? What do you want?" Majnun called when he saw the visitor approaching.

"I am Salim from the tribe of the Banu Amir—Salim, your uncle."

Majnun recognized him and ordered his animals to allow the visitor to enter. He asked after all his family and Salim saw that Majnun had not lost his senses. He begged Majnun to put on a robe, for it pained him to see Majnun naked.

At his uncle's insistence, he agreed, but the food that his uncle offered to him he gave to his animals. "I no longer deserve food," he told Salim. "Grass and a few roots are all I wish, but I thank you for your gifts to my animals."

"Perhaps you are right," Salim said. "Birds are caught in traps because they are greedy, and the greedier the human the more he is in danger. There is a story about such things—the story of the king and the dervish. . . .

"Once a great king rode past the hut of a hermit. It was a miserable, crumbling hut and he asked his advisor, 'Who can live in such a place?'

"The advisor said, 'A holy man lives there who needs neither food nor water.'

"The king was curious and said, 'Let us go back. I want to speak to this man.'

"When the hermit was brought to the king, the advisor asked him, 'Where do you find the strength to endure such misery? How do you live? What do you eat?'

" 'Here is my dinner,' the hermit said happily, and he showed them some plants he had found on the plains.

" 'What misery!' the courtier said. 'If you entered the service of the king, you would certainly have better food than grass.'

" 'Grass?' the hermit cried. 'Sir, this isn't grass. This is honey blossoms. If you knew how good it tastes, you would leave the king's service this instant.'

"The king understood. He embraced the hermit and said, 'Only someone who is content with very little is free.' That is my story, Majnun," his uncle concluded. "Some may take you for a madman, but to me you are as wise as the wisest of kings."

Majnun thanked his uncle for the story, and for a time he was almost cheerful. But then, suddenly, he thought of his mother. For so long he had not thought of her. But now he asked how she was and said that he longed to see her beauty again.

"I will bring her to you," Salim said.

In a week, Salim returned with Majnun's mother. For a moment, when she saw her son from afar, her heart shrank. But then she rushed past lion, panther, and wolf to her son and kissed him and caressed him. And only after she had combed his tangled hair and washed and tended his wounds did she speak. "Oh, my son, you are still drunk with the wine of your youth. Why do you sleep in caves among ants and snakes? The snakes will bite you. The ants will eat you. Come to your senses. Life is brief. It passes as quickly as two days. Your father is dead, and I do not know how many days are given to me."

"My mother, my beautiful mother, forgive me," Majnun said. "Let your life be long. I know you are unhappy because I suffer. I did not choose it. We are each given a portion. But even if I were to return home, I would die, for that home is a prison to me. You want to free the bird of the soul from the cage. But the cage is my home. The cage is my love. Mother, forgive me, forgive me for giving you pain. I cannot help it."

Majnun kissed his mother's feet and begged her forgiveness. His mother wept and set out for home with her brother. But now her home became foreign to her, for her home was with Majnun. A short time later, she died.

Majnun's uncle visited Majnun to tell him of his mother's death. Majnun battered his face and beat the ground like glass hitting a stone. He hurried to where his mother was buried. He wailed and lamented. When his relatives saw Majnun's despair, they asked him to stay, but Majnun ran from them to his cave and his animals. His grief needed the expanse of the sky.

During this time, Layla waited for a response from Majnun. Night after night she slipped from her tent and walked to the crossroads, watching for the old man. One evening as she approached the crossroads, she saw a shadow in front of her and knew it was the old man. "Tell me," she whispered, "what news do you bring of my wild love? What does he say? What does he dream about?"

"He says your name," the old man answered. "He whispers your name. He speaks your name. He shouts your name. 'Layla! Layla!' " And the old man gave her Majnun's letter.

Layla read the letter and said, "I beg you, I must see him." Then she loosened some pearls from her earrings and gave them to the old man, saying, "Bring Majnun to me. Let me see his face. I want one glance of light. And perhaps he will recite a few lines that will unravel the twisted skein of my soul."

The old man soon returned with Majnun. Majnun's animals waited in the grove, and Majnun, after putting on the robe the old man offered him, went trembling to Layla's garden.

Almost at once Layla came out of her tent wrapped in a veil. She saw Majnun leaning against a tree. He was ten steps away, but she could not go up to him. She stood rooted to the earth. Layla turned to the old man and whispered, "I cannot go any farther. If I do, I will be consumed. Ask Majnun to speak. He will be the cupbearer. I will drink the wine."

The old man went to the quiet figure by the tree and realized that Majnun had just fainted. He gently lifted Majnun up and held him until he awoke. When Majnun opened his eyes and saw Layla gazing at him, he offered her the verses she had asked for.

Layla listened but she did not answer. Then Majnun sang the most beautiful song of his life:

> "In heaven we are joined.
> On earth we are apart.
> Not death or fear or decay can separate our hearts.
>
> Our souls wander freely
> and choose for all eternity
> to combine.
> Mine is yours. Yours is mine."

After a time, Majnun was silent. Layla, too, was silent. Then Majnun fled from Layla's garden.

When Majnun returned to his cave, a young man by the name of Salam from Baghdad was waiting for him. He had been wounded in love and had journeyed to the wilderness to hear Majnun's verses.

"Where do you come from?" Majnun asked the boy.

"From journey's end," the boy answered. And when he looked at Majnun, who stood naked, surrounded by his animals, he said, "I want to be your slave. I want to serve you and listen to you and guard you and never leave your side. I have been crushed by the millstone of love. I want to hear your songs."

"Go home," Majnun said. "Your place is not with me. You have not tasted my sufferings. I cannot provide for you. I have nothing but my creatures. Even the demons flee from me. What do you want? You are your own friend. I am not human. I am savage. I destroy myself."

"For God's sake," the boy persisted, "do not refuse my thirst. Let me drink from your well. I am a pilgrim. And you are Mecca."

Majnun let him stay. The boy then took from his bag all kinds of delicacies and spread them on a rug before Majnun, saying, "Be my guest. Eat for your strength. Do not feed on despair alone. Even the sky is not the same but changes, revealing new pages in the Book of Life. Do not be so faithful to your sorrow. I also was broken by love. But God helped me. Laugh! Play! In the end, your grief will be lessened and you will forget."

Majnun held his anger and said, "I am no lovesick fool. I do not crave satisfaction. My body no longer has desire. Love is my fire and essence. The bundle which is my self is gone. Love has entered my house. You do not see me. You see 'the beloved.' How then can love be torn from my heart?"

The youth repented his careless words. He stayed with Majnun, collecting his verses and accepting the desert life. But after a time, he could not endure so many weeks without sleep or food.

He returned to Baghdad, and as he traveled through the villages, he sang Majnun's songs, and the people who listened copied down his poems. And when they knew love themselves, it was with Majnun's words that they sang, for Majnun spoke for lovers everywhere.

In the Book of Life, every page has two sides. On one side are our hopes and aspirations. On the other side, what is destined for us. Rarely are the two sides the same. Our satisfaction can well be our peril, and our difficulties our salvation. The meaning is there, but it is hard to grasp. Vinegar can prove to be honey, and honey, vinegar.

Layla's husband possessed the jewel he desired. And yet, his possession was an illusion. Zealously, he guarded the treasure to which no path could lead him. Layla rarely asked to see him. She was his wife, but she remained a bride.

It was Layla's husband, Ibni Salam, who let go first. Was it fate which released him? Or was it the burden of loving without being loved?

One day, he was suddenly taken ill with a violent fever. The doctor was summoned and gave him healing potions, and he recovered. But as soon as the doctor left, he ate the foods the doctor had forbidden him, and he fell ill again. This time the doctor was helpless. Although Ibni Salam was young, in a few days his soul fled from his body and he died.

Ibni Salam was dead. Layla pitied her husband, but mostly she felt relief. At last, she was free to weep without restraint. She went into seclusion and wept as a widow might, and no one knew she wept for Majnun.

She performed this ritual until autumn when the trees blazed with color and the wind rose. During her many months of solitude she became weak. Then a fever took her, and knowing she would die, she called her mother to her tent and revealed her secret for the first time.

"Oh Mother, I am fading away. And what has my life been? I have suffered so much in secret. I must speak to you now. The grief in my heart is breaking the seal on my lips. Listen to me, Mother. I am like an autumn leaf on a branch of the Tree of Life. When I die, dress me in my bridal robes, so I may receive my beloved as a bride. I know my restless wanderer will come to my grave. Oh Mother, I have loved him, and my wish is that you too will love him.

"When you see my beloved, comfort him as you would comfort me. Speak to him and tell him that when I left the world, I did so thinking of him. Tell him that his grief has always been mine and I have taken it with me to sustain me on my journey. He cannot see my eyes. But tell him that I will be following him and waiting and asking, 'Beloved, when do you come?' "

Tears streamed down Layla's face. She spoke her beloved's name, and she passed the frontier to the other land. Her mother clasped her to her and tried to breathe life into her. She tore her own white hair and wept and shouted. But to no avail. Even if heaven laments, each must cross the threshold alone.

As Layla foretold, when Majnun heard of her death, he came like a thundercloud driven by a storm. He fell on her grave as if he had been struck by lightning. Writhing and twisting in torment, he cried, "Layla! Layla! What do you see? What do your gazelle's eyes see? Where is your amber-scented hair? Where have you melted? In which bowl? Are you in a cave? Where there are caves, there are serpents, live serpents. I am your serpent. I have no other home."

Then Majnun jumped up and fled to the wilderness, weeping and singing, followed by his animals. But as soon as he came to his cave, he ran back to Layla's grave and covered the earth with kisses.

For a month, Majnun stayed at Layla's grave, guarded by his animals. No one dared to approach him. Day by day he grew weaker. At last the day came when he had no more strength. That evening, he lifted his hands to the sky and prayed, "Creator of all things, I beg you, in the name of all you have created, release me from my torment. Let me go to my love. She is waiting."

Then Majnun lay his head on the earth, held Layla's gravestone, and spoke his last words: "You . . . my love. . . ."

For many months, no one knew of Majnun's death, for his animals guarded his body with fierce growls. But when his body had crumbled to dust, they went back to the wilderness.

Then Majnun's tribesmen came and gathered his bones and buried them by Layla's side. All that day and for many days after, there was mourning in the camp of the Banu Amir and in the camp of Layla's people.

Since their deaths, their story has been told and retold, for never have there been two lovers as true as they.

TRISTAN AND ISEULT

One Man, One Woman

for Hugh Van Dusen

My friends, proceed with caution. This is a dark story, and I would not wish you to suffer such a fate as Tristan and Iseult. But you protest, "Where is there joy without sorrow? Where is there ecstasy without pain?" And I say, "Beware! Beware of love!"

But you will not listen to me because I am a fool. You will do what we all do. You will try to find out for yourself, and that is very foolish. Remember—I have warned you!

And now I am free to ponder the masks and mysteries of the story. Slowly then, I will unravel for you the thread, the double thread containing:

One man, one woman, one woman, one man.
Tristan, Iseult, Iseult, Tristan.

In the time of the troubadours, long ago, in a castle in Parmenie, an orphan was raised secretly by a vassal. The orphan was a young lord, and his vassal, the faithful Rual li Foitenant, wishing to protect the young lord, brought him up as his own son and never told him he was the peer of princes. The boy's name was Tristan, which means sadness.

Now I warned you this would be a sad story.

Tristan's father, Rivalen of Parmenie, had been killed in battle. His mother, the beautiful Blanchefleur, had died after giving birth to him.

Sad, sad, sad, all very sad.

Rual and his wife, Florette, treated Tristan as one of their own sons. In fact, as was his due, they treated him better. When Tristan was seven, they hired special tutors to train him in the arts of languages, music, knightly sports, and falconry. Tristan excelled at everything he did. He had all the gifts anyone could ever wish for. He was wonderful to look at, kind, generous, wise, and had perfect manners. His mother so doted on him that if she could she would have covered the path he walked on with velvet.

When Tristan was fourteen, a Norwegian merchant ship, filled with a rich cargo of jewels, silks, and falcons, anchored near the castle of Canoel. Tristan's brothers, who wanted to buy falcons for sport, begged Tristan to speak to their father, for they knew their father would never refuse Tristan anything he asked.

At Tristan's urging, they went to the ship and bought seven white falcons. As they were leaving, Tristan noticed an exquisitely carved ivory chess set and asked if the merchants wanted to play. The Norwegians were intrigued by this young lad, with his fine face and manners, who was the only one in his family who could speak their language.

"Yes," they said, "we'll take you on."

Rual left Tristan in the care of his tutor, Govenal, and returned to the castle with his other sons. Tristan played game after game, and each game he played he won. The merchants marveled at this boy. Not only did he speak German, English, and Latin, but between games he sang with the loveliest of voices. The merchants eyed each other. What a price they would get if they were to sell the boy. Then one of the merchants silently gestured to the sailors to lift anchor, and the ship drifted out of the bay.

Tristan and Govenal were so engrossed in the game that not until the wind came up did Tristan turn from the game and see that they were far from the shore. "Where are you taking us?" he cried.

"To your new home in Norway!" they answered. "Be glad and make merry!"

"NO!" Tristan wailed.

"NO!!" Govenal cried. *"NO!! NO-OOO!!!"* The noise of their wailing was so deafening that the sailors put Govenal in a small skiff with one oar and pushed it off from the ship.

Govenal at once alerted the steward, Rual, who ran down to the sea followed by his household. No ship was in sight. "Tristan, my life! My delight! How will I live without you? Heavenly father protect the boy!" Rual cried. And he wept uncontrollably. Tristan's brothers, who had often been envious of him, now wept for him and for their father. Florette, too, wept and prayed for her son and her lord.

Tristan did not stop his wailing. The sky changed. Great waves rose up from the sea. Lightning flashed across the sky. Rain and hail pummeled the ship. After eight days, the sailors, in terror, begged the captain to release the boy. The moment the captain agreed, the waters became calm, and the storm ended. As soon as they saw land, they put Tristan ashore and sailed away.

Tristan looked about him. He did not know where he was. All he saw were crags and cliffs and the raging sea.

What did he do? Why, what any child would do. He wept. He wept. Oh, he wept.

He wept until he was done, and then he prayed to God to protect him in this unknown land, and cursing the game he had to win and the falcons he had to buy, he lifted his brocade cloak and slowly made his way up the rough face of the cliff.

At the top of the cliff, he met two old pilgrims, barefooted and chanting, who were on their way to Tintagel. When they questioned him, Tristan cautiously explained that he had become separated from his hunting party. The pilgrims invited him to accompany them.

Tristan walked with them for a time, when suddenly a hart leapt across their path into a stream. Hunting dogs pursued the hart, followed by horns, boys, and the chief huntsman. The hart came out of the water and the dogs attacked it. As the huntsman was about to quarter the prey, Tristan went up to him and said, "Sir, if you permit me, I will show you a cleaner, easier way to dress the hart."

The huntsman looked at the young man in his green brocade cloak with a white ermine lining and thought, Before me stands either a foreign squire or a baron. "Sir," the huntsman said, "I would be pleased if you would show me your method, for I know only this way."

Tristan took the offered knife and with expert skill, stripped, cut, and dressed the hart, handing back to the huntsman not many bloody pieces, ripped by the dogs, but one entire skin. The huntsman was delighted and said, "Young man, I will take you to court and present you to the king."

Tristan's fortune begins with the hunt, for he is a great hunter. His skill brings him fortune, and his skill brings him misfortune. In the end the hunter is the one who flees. But that is the end, and we are at the beginning, and Tristan is on his way to Tintagel . . .

The chief huntsman gave Tristan a horse and a hunting horn; and as they rode to Tintagel, Tristan told them that he was the son of a merchant from Parmenie who, eager for adventure, had run off to sea. He played lively hunting tunes which the young boys echoed on their horns. They entered Tintagel and the halls of the castle filled with music. The king appeared, and for a moment Tristan's heart swelled and he was silent. Then he bowed to the king, played a special melody, and cried in French, "God save the king and all the court!" The huntsman presented Tristan of Parmenie to King Mark, and the king was drawn to this boy, with his clear eyes, his fine form, and his radiance.

Several nights later, Tristan sat at the king's feet and listened as a Welsh minstrel played. After one of the songs, Tristan spoke with the minstrel. The minstrel then insisted that Tristan play. Tristan retuned the harp, and soon his slender fingers danced across the strings bringing forth such delight that some in the room who listened forgot their own names, while others ran from the room to bring their friends. King Mark observed this merchant's son from Parmenie and thought of his own sister, Blanchefleur, who so many years ago had gone away to Parmenie.

Mark called for song after song. Tristan sang in Irish, in Breton, in Welsh, in Latin, and in French. When he had finished, the members of the household questioned him, and Tristan answered each courteously in his own language. Everyone marveled at this fourteen-year-old boy who had such talents and yet was so modest. "Oh, Tristan, how fortunate you are. What a glorious life you will lead!"

The king said, "Tristan, you shall stay at court and be my companion. In the day we shall hunt and ride; and at night you will play on the harp and sing. You will do for me what you do well; in return, I will do what I know well. I will give you all the fine clothes and horses your heart desires. Tristan, you have brought great joy to our household. I entrust you with my sword, my spurs, my bow, and my golden horn. Guard them well and be a merry courtier!"

And so Tristan came to live at Tintagel and became the court favorite. He knew the art of friendship. He was willing to live for others. He laughed. He sang. He danced. He rode. And whatever he did, he did with great happiness and affection.

During this time, the faithful Rual was searching for Tristan. He had crossed the seas to Norway to look for his young lord. From Norway, he went to Ireland. He spent the gold he had brought and was forced to send his vassals home. Then he begged for bread to live. At last, in the fourth year, in Denmark, he came across two old pilgrims who described having met just such a young lord who was wearing a green brocade cloak with a white ermine lining and was on his way to Tintagel.

"To Tintagel?" Rual cried in astonishment. "If he was on his way to Tintagel, then he was on his way home, for Mark is his own uncle!" He thanked the pilgrims and set out for Cornwall without resting. But when he came to Tintagel, he did not dare enter. His clothes were torn. He had no shoes. His hair and beard were matted. He waited outside the castle until an old courtier appeared. Rual went up to him and humbly asked, "Sir, do you know of a page at court by the name of Tristan?"

"Oh, not a page," the courtier corrected him, "but a young squire, the king's favorite, soon to be knighted for his many accomplishments."

"As a great kindness to me," Rual asked, "can you tell the squire that a poor man from his country waits outside to see him?"

Tristan soon appeared. When he saw Rual, he threw his arms in the air and shouted and ran to him and hugged and kissed him and laughed with gladness. "Father, Father!" he cried, and he hugged him and kissed him again and said, "Father, oh but Father, what has happened to you? And where is my mother? And where are my brothers?"

"I cannot tell you," Rual said, "for I have been searching for you all these years, and I have had no word from them."

"Oh Father, you must meet the king, and the king must meet you." Although he protested, in moments Rual found himself in his threadbare robe, with no shoes or cloak, standing before King Mark.

Tristan said, "Your Majesty, this is my father. He has the look of a poor man, but that is because he has been traveling for many years through many lands searching for me. I would be glad if you would greet him well."

Mark welcomed Rual cordially and ordered that a bath and clothes be prepared for him. That evening, bathed and finely attired, Rual sat at the table with Mark and the court. Tristan sat across from his father, gazing at him with happy eyes.

"Tell us of your journey. Tell us of your country and your family," Mark asked Rual.

"Sire, I have had no news of my family. Four years ago I left my wife and three sons to search for this boy who is not my son."

"Not your son?" Mark said, "Then why does he call you father?"

"I am his servant, not his father."

"Then tell us of this marvel."

"Sire, lords and ladies, my lord was Rivalen of Parmenie. I do not know if you remember this noble knight who came to your court many years ago. He was the greatest of knights—brave, generous, handsome, loyal. He gave joy to all who were in his company. He had only one fault: his arrogance. He had a dreadful temper and could never forgive a wrong. He was always warring with his neighbor, the arrogant Breton Duke Morgan. Well, at a time when a truce was declared between Morgan and

Rivalen, Rivalen decided to journey to Tintagel to perfect himself in the arts of chivalry.

"That May, Mark's vassals traveled from all over England for a month of festivities. On grassy meadows, under lime trees and leafy arbors, knights and garlanded ladies set up their tents and silk pavilions. There was music and dancing and feasting, clowns and jugglers and fools. Certain knights met in counsel with the king. Others paraded in the newest fashions; and still others competed in jousting, fencing, and wrestling.

"Blanchefleur told me that the knight who outshone all the others was Rivalen of Parmenie. The court ladies watched him compete and whispered among themselves, 'How magnificent his legs are!' 'How elegant his clothes!' 'How fortunate the woman who will have her pleasure with him!'

"Blanchefleur heard what the others said, but it was not her ears as much as her eyes that were caught. The sight of Rivalen entered her heart, where he took over her heart's crown and scepter.

"After the tournaments, each knight galloped in the direction of his fancy. Rivalen rode up to King Mark's sister, bowed, and said, 'God bless you, lovely lady.'

"Blanchefleur answered, 'And may God who gladdens all hearts gladden yours. But you have hurt a friend of mine, the best I ever had.' Rivalen imagined that he had unwittingly injured a kinsperson of hers in the past. But no, the friend she was referring to was her heart.

" 'Lovely Lady, I would in no way wish to harm you,' Rivalen said. 'State your command and I will do as you wish.'

" 'Another time,' Blanchefleur said with a sigh, 'I will test you another time.'

"Then Blanchefleur languished for the knight from Parmenie for she did not know if he cared for her or not. He had taken her heart, and when she imagined that he was stealing other women's hearts as well, she despised him. But as her sweet pain did not lessen and her longing grew, she realized that what she felt for Rivalen was what she had heard about all her life. She loved him. He was her destiny. So the next time he looked at her, she did not lower her eyes but gazed steadfastly back at him. And Rivalen let her enter his heart, where he crowned her queen.

"Soon after this, Rivalen was called off to battle to help the king. In the first fight Rivalen was injured. The other ladies pitied the handsome knight who would never again compete in the tournaments. But Blanchefleur disguised herself as a woman physician and went to his room. When the others left, she knelt by his bedside. His eyes were dim and unseeing. She placed her lips on his. She kissed him. She kissed him a hundred thousand times. At last her love aroused him. He pulled her to him and they had their way with each other. From that union a child was conceived.

"Rivalen recovered and they lived together in bliss. For Rivalen there was Blanchefleur, for Blanchefleur there was Rivalen. He was she, she was he. They would not have exchanged what they lived on earth for any heavenly kingdom. Then, in the midst of their joy, Duke Morgan invaded Rivalen's lands. A messenger was sent to inform Rivalen. I was the one who sent the messenger.

"Rivalen went to speak with Blanchefleur. He spoke to her curtly. 'Lovely lady, I must sail home. God protect you. Stay happy and be well always.' She caught her breath and sobbed, 'Woe! Woe for love! How short its joy. How long its sorrow. You have given me a child, and now you would leave me in shame and dishonor.'

"Then, he lost his composure and he too wept and said, 'No, dearest lady, I will not leave you. You have given me your heart and the greatest happiness I have known. I would never wish to cause you pain. It is my wish that we share the future together, whether it is joy or sorrow. You choose. Let your heart choose. Shall I stay here in Cornwall with you? Or will you sail to Parmenie with me?'

"She chose to sail with her beloved to Parmenie. They were married by the clergy, and then Rivalen gave Blanchefleur into my keeping. In all my life, I have never seen such a beautiful woman.

"Rivalen rode off to gather his vassals. He attacked Duke Morgan. The fighting went on for weeks. It was long, fierce, and brutal. In the worst of the fighting, my lord was killed. His men, who loved him, gave him cover and took him from the battle. We mourned him with great sorrow.

"But when Blanchefleur heard that Rivalen was dead, she turned mute. May all you who are listening to my story be spared such pain. Blanchefleur went into labor and for three days and three nights did not utter a sound or a moan. On the fourth day, she gave birth to a child, a little boy. 'Sad, sad little man,' she said, and she named him Tristan. Then she died. My wife took the infant from her arms. And I took the ring from her finger to give to her son when he would be old enough to have his own sword and avenge his father's death." Then Rual paused in his story.

Yes, and it was time he paused; for if a story goes on too long, we become confused as to just which story we are in. This was the state Tristan was in.

Tristan was stunned. In one moment he was an orphan; in the next moment he had a mother, Florette, and two fathers, Rual and the king. Rual found the ring in his pouch and presented it to Mark, who recognized it at once as the ring his father had given to him that he had given to Blanchefleur. Mark wept. Then all the court rose and kissed and welcomed the noble Rual.

Tristan did not move. He sat there speechless. Rual, noticing

Tristan's confusion, went to him and shook him and said, "Tristan, you are not alone. You are in a room with both your fathers. Ask your father, the king, to knight you so that you can return home to reclaim your fief."

At last Tristan came to his senses. He knelt before Mark and said, "Your Majesty, I beg you, knight me and give me thirty companions to help me avenge my father's death. Let me be knighted in proper style. And let God bestow sufficient property on me that I might gain great wealth and honor."

King Mark looked at the handsome youth with pride. He had loved him before he knew he was his nephew. "Tristan, I will knight you and give you thirty companions. And more than that, I will be your father's successor and make you my heir. Go to Parmenie, settle your affairs to your advantage and honor, and come back quickly, for I will not marry. I will wait for you. You will be the next king of England and Cornwall!"

A month later, Tristan and his thirty companions were knighted and came from Mass carrying their newly consecrated swords. Mark blessed him and said, "Now that your sword is consecrated, remember your knightly duties. Do not forget your birth and nobility. Be proud before the mighty; be merciful to the poor. Take care for your appearance. Honor all women; help any who are in need. Be modest, truthful, and straightforward. Above all, be generous and loyal." Then he gave Tristan his mother's ring and a gold shield engraved with the sign of the wild boar.

With thirty knighted companions and sixty other knights whom Mark had entrusted to him, Tristan returned to Parmenie with Rual. He greeted his mother and brothers with great joy. Then he gathered together his vassals, and when they had given their allegiance, he spoke to them of his mission to wrest his realm from Duke Morgan.

Several months later, Tristan heard that Morgan was hunting in the woods not far from Parmenie. He alerted his knights. Thirty rode with him, their cloaks covering their swords. Sixty were to follow. When Tristan approached Duke Morgan, Morgan greeted him courteously as he might any stranger. But when Tristan said, "I am Tristan of Parmenie. I have come to reclaim my fief," Morgan laughed in his face and said, *"Your* fief? Why boy, you've not even the right to carry a sword! You're a bastard and all the country knows it! Your mother never married your father. If you want your land, go to the devil! He's holding it for you!"

In a fury, Tristan drew his sword from under his cloak and split Morgan's skull, separating it down to the tongue. Morgan's companions attacked. Tristan's knights threw off their cloaks and fought back. They fought all day. The earth was soon covered with skulls and blood and swords. Morgan's countrymen arrived throughout the night and would have outnumbered Tristan's forces if Rual had not appeared at dawn with his own and Tristan's vassals. To the cries of "Chevaliers Parmenie!" they attacked and defeated the Bretons.

Tristan was then given great honor for having reclaimed his fief. But now what was he to do? He had two fathers who both loved him. Was he to stay in Parmenie? Or was he to return to Cornwall?

Tristan chose to divide his property from his person. He gave his wealth and his revenues to his father, Rual, and, upon his death, his fief to Rual's sons. Then, he returned to Cornwall with Govenal. Rual sadly watched Tristan depart. No man ever inherited a fief with greater sorrow than Rual. He longed for Tristan to remain in Parmenie, and yet he knew that Tristan merited the honor he would receive at Mark's court.

When Tristan and Govenal crossed the seas to Cornwall, they witnessed woeful scenes of weeping. Mothers and children were weeping in the streets. In the castle, no one greeted Tristan. The great barons were on their knees, praying and weeping, imploring God to spare their offspring. It was the time of the solstice, and for five years now, King Gurmun had demanded tribute from Cornwall and England. The first year it was bronze, the next year, silver, the third year, gold, and the fourth year, sixty of the finest sons of the land. This was the fifth year, and King Gurmun of Ireland had sent his brother-in-law, ruthless Morholt, to again bring back sixty young men of Cornwall.

Tristan walked boldly to the head of the hall where King Mark and Morholt were about to draw lots. Tristan spoke loudly for all to hear: "Barons! Lords! Have you forgotten who you are? You are the equals of kings, the peers of princes! Would you sell your sons—your very lives—into slavery? God would not have you sell your children into slavery. Is there not one among you who dares to face Morholt? Choose one man, pray for him, and let him face Morholt in single combat."

"Oh Tristan," the men nearest to him spoke. "Morholt has the strength and power of four men. He is pitiless. No one man can fight him."

"Then you *have* forgotten your births! If no one dares to risk his life to end the weeping in Cornwall, in God's name, I will take on the combat for all of you. Our towns and fortresses have been leveled, but now we are strong enough in both men and wealth to stand on our own!" And although Mark tried to dissuade him, Tristan threw his glove at Morholt's feet.

Morholt stood up. He towered over Tristan. He looked down at him and said, "I have often heard such boasting. A treaty was made long ago of force or tribute. If you refuse tribute, since there are not enough men with me to ride to war in proper defense, I will meet you in three days' time at the Isle of Saint

Samson in single combat." And he gave Tristan his glove.

Three days later, Morholt beached his purple skiff at the Isle of Saint Samson. Soon after, Tristan arrived and pushed his boat out to sea, brashly proclaiming, "Only one boat is needed. Only one of us will survive."

The two knights mounted their horses and charged. They flew at each other with such speed that each knight's spear was splintered on the other's shield. Then they drew out their swords and fought from the saddle, blow by blow, parry by parry. It was a glorious fight until Morholt fell on Tristan like a thunderclap and let loose such a rain of blows that Tristan thrust his shield too far from his side, and Morholt struck him in the thigh, wounding him. Blood rushed to the ground.

"Give it up, vassal!" Morholt cried. "You can see for yourself your cause is not just. You are beaten! My sword is coated with deadly poison, and there is no one who can cure you but my sister, the queen of Ireland. If you admit your wrong, I will take you home and share with you all I have, for I have never met a knight who pleased me more than you."

Tristan replied, "I will not give up my honor or the freedom of my country for you or your sister. The tribute is your death or mine. Let God restore justice!"

Then Tristan, sensing God's presence, which was greater than four or eight or twelve men, beat his thighs like wings and crashed into Morholt's charger. Morholt fell from his charger; his helmet flew from his head. He covered his back with his shield, but before he could reach his helmet, Tristan struck him. The blow was so fierce that when Tristan withdrew his sword, a fragment of steel remained embedded in Morholt's skull. Tristan then took Morholt's sword in both his hands and struck off his enemy's head.

Tristan returned in the purple skiff. Loud cheers arose when the Irish saw the purple skiff, but as soon as the boat drew closer and Tristan was seen at the helm, those who were rejoicing fell to keening while those who had been weeping began to sing loud songs of praise.

Joy and sorrow. Sorrow and joy. The English and the Irish. The Irish and the English. Up and down. Down and up. Around and around. And here is much of our story: One man's sorrow is another man's joy. One woman's joy is another woman's sorrow. A-las-sy, alassy, aladdie. Aladdie, aladdie, alas!

Sadly, the Irish collected their hero and brought him home. The king ordered that all people landing in Ireland from Cornish ships should be hung without mercy. The queen, despite her fame in healing, could do nothing. Still, she plucked the steel splinter from Morholt's skull and placed it in an iron box so that she would not forget the name of the man who had murdered her brother.

Tristan was loved and lauded throughout England and Cornwall. Single-handedly he had restored his country's honor. Yet the words Morholt had spoken were true. No doctor could cure him. His wound turned color and gave off such a stench that his body became a burden to him and only the king and Govenal could bear to be near him.

Remembering Morholt's words, Tristan asked his uncle's leave to sail to Ireland. At first, Mark resisted. "Wait," he counseled, "Who can know what can happen in a day? One day can change a year's movement." But as the days passed and Tristan's sufferings increased, Mark reluctantly agreed. Weeping, he accompanied Tristan to the boat. Tristan departed secretly with Govenal and six trusted sailors. When they were within sight of

Dublin, the sailors placed Tristan in a small skiff, and Tristan ordered Govenal to return quickly to Cornwall so no harm would come to them. He advised Govenal to tell his uncle that if he were destined to recover he would do so within a year, but everyone else was to be informed that he was dead, and Govenal was to pay the sailors well to keep his secret.

Tristan drifted. He had no oar or sail or sword. He had only his harp and rations for three days. He lay on his back and watched the sky. A strong living tune came to him. He fingered his harp and sang.

Fishermen nearby thought they heard angels singing. Looking about, they saw a solitary boat tossing from wave to wave. They rowed closer and found a lifeless young man still plucking the strings of his harp. They carried him to their queen and told her that the wounded man played like a choir of angels singing. The queen washed the wound with her own hands. She drew out the poison, set a special poultice on it, and waited.

Ten days later, the wounded man opened his eyes.

"Tell me, minstrel," the queen said, "what is your name? And where are you from?"

"I am Tantris," he said. "Tantris the minstrel, from Spain. I could play fiddle and lyre, harp and dulcimer. I could jest and joke and sing. And all was well with me until my head was turned by desires for wealth, and foolishly, oh, so foolishly, I thought to advance myself by becoming a merchant. Pirates attacked our ship and only spared my life because of my harp."

"I too have spared your life because of your song," the queen said. "I have a daughter, and I would have you teach her to play and to sing." As she spoke, the young Iseult entered. She was so beautiful that when Tristan saw her, his life returned. He took up his harp. His fingers danced across the strings, and he played better than he had ever played in his life.

And so it was that for six months Tristan came to live in the women's quarters of the palace. Every day he tutored the princess. He taught her the arts of courtesy. He taught her to read and to write and to sing. He set his learning before her and let her choose which instruments and songs she would learn.

The princess mastered all that the minstrel taught her and soon was composing songs and reading and singing her own compositions for her father's court. Her sweet voice delighted those who listened, while her secret song, which was her extraordinary beauty, caused their hearts to leap with wild and unexpected desires. The queen and princess came to love the Spanish minstrel and wished that he would stay forever. But Tristan, fearing that he would be recognized, and knowing that he had to return within a year, said that he had to sail for Spain or his wife might think him dead and take another husband.

Sadly, the queen and Iseult watched him leave. Yet if they had known his true name, they would have happily hacked him into pieces.

Tristan returned to Cornwall and all he could speak of was the beautiful Iseult: "She is dazzling! She is radiant!" he told the court. "Until now I had thought that the beauty of women dwelt in Greece with Helen, but now I know where to look to see the sun rise. To Ireland and to Iseult! Anyone who stands in her presence becomes more beautiful. If she but glances into your eyes, you feel your soul melt like gold in a white-hot flame."

Tristan, of course, was exaggerating. But perhaps not. Perhaps the natural beauty of a woman is beyond compare. Well, if so, shhh! Let the tongue hunger and the eye feast. Boasting fills neither the belly nor the soul. But if you must speak, speak of me! No one enjoys praise as much as a fool!

The barons heard and the king heard. And after Tristan's return, some of the barons, whether from envy or greed or fear, began to speak against Tristan. Tristan asked the king to speak with them regarding their intentions, but Mark assured Tristan, saying, "It is only because of your worth that they are envious. Worth and envy are mother and child. In time worth always bears envy. Do not concern yourself with them. You are my heir."

"Then I will be forced to leave the court," Tristan replied. "I cannot rule the land with such enmity. I beg you, listen to your advisors and ask their intentions so we can settle this matter."

Mark, who wished to please Tristan, summoned the barons. Andret, the king's nephew, spoke for the others. "Sire, as your barons, we have been considering what is needed to safeguard the kingdom. It is our opinion that a proper heir is needed. We advise you to choose a wife."

"Heaven has given us an heir," Mark answered. "We must keep him alive. While Tristan lives, there will be no queen at court."

The malice of the barons then increased to such an extent that Tristan, fearing for his life, told his uncle he had no choice but to leave the court. "Of what use would it be to me to rule the whole earth if I am to live in fear?"

Once again, to mollify Tristan, Mark summoned his barons and asked them their opinion.

"The woman we advise you to choose for a wife," they said, "is the one Tristan has so extolled—Iseult the Fair, Iseult of the Golden Hair, Iseult, the princess of Ireland!"

"Well, I, too, have thought of her," said Mark. "But you know how much we are hated by her father and her people. How would you bring about such a match?"

"Send Tristan! He speaks their language. He is prudent, he is ambitious, *and* he knows witchcraft! How else did he return from Ireland unharmed?"

"What evil festers in your hearts!" Mark cried. "No man is more hated in Ireland than Tristan. Tristan has already risked his life for you. No, no, my vassals, if you wish Cornwall to have an heir, you must go yourselves!"

Tristan then understood the barons' intentions and said, "Sire, they are right. Let me go. I am the one to represent you, for I speak their language, and I want it to be known that I, too, wish an heir for England and Cornwall."

Mark protested, "Tristan, I would not have you risk your life a second time in Ireland."

"But it is the only way. Let me go, and let those who speak ill of me go with me. God will then decide if I am to blame that Cornwall is without an heir."

So Tristan set sail with a cargo of fine clothes, holy relics, and forty barons dressed as merchants and sixty mercenaries. The barons were miserable; in fact, in all their lives, they had never been so miserable. They cursed the hour they had ever conceived such plans, but having provoked their own fate they were now forced to count on Tristan to save their lives.

Isn't that like so many of us, proposing a journey for others that we would little wish to undertake ourselves?

When they reached the harbor at Wexford, Tristan covered his face with a hood which men often wear on a journey. He ordered his men to stay below and refused, despite their many requests, to reveal his intentions. He set Govenal in charge and suggested that if he did not return in four days they go back to England and choose another wife for their king. When the marshall of the harbor arrived to investigate, Tristan presented him with a handsome gold goblet to secure a safe stay for their "Flemish merchant ship bound for Spain."

In the morning, terrifying cries awoke the ship. Tristan went out into the street and saw men, women, and children fleeing from a dreadful dragon who daily entered the city, killing and frightening the people. Since the death of Morholt, no knight had been able to kill the dragon. King Gurmun had made an offer of his daughter in marriage to any man of noble birth who could slay the dragon.

Tristan, who had known of this offer before he set out from Cornwall, mounted a sturdy warhorse, armed himself with a stout spear and rode at once in the direction of the cries. Three knights galloping in terror from the dragon's lair motioned to him to turn back, but Tristan eagerly spurred his horse and rode faster.

As he came near the dragon, he saw scorched grass. Then he saw smoke and flames, and there rose up before him a huge dragon. Fire and venom spewed out of the dragon's eyes and tongue. The dragon turned toward him. Tristan readied his spear, spurred his horse, and charged. The spear tore through the dragon's throat and split its heart. The dragon fell with a great roar, and then it rose again and charged at Tristan. Tristan leapt from his horse and the dragon devoured half of the horse up to the saddle. Then Tristan, despite the heat of the flames, plunged his sword into the dragon's heart a second time. The dragon let out a horrific cry, which sounded as if heaven and earth were falling, and sank to the ground, dead. Tristan cut off the dragon's tongue and limped away.

When the king of Ireland's ambitious steward heard the dragon's death cry, he rode at once to the lair. At the sight of the half-eaten horse, he fled. But since no dragon pursued him, he stopped, remounted his horse, and cautiously rode back to the lair. This time he rode a little farther, saw the dead dragon, and guessing that the one who had killed the dragon had been killed by the dragon, he bravely thrust his spear into the dead dragon's head, staking his claim. He tried to cut off the head with his sword, but the neck was too thick. So he broke his spear on a log, plunged half of it in the dragon's jaw, and galloped back to town, brandishing his bloody spear and shouting, "Your Majesty, I have slain the dragon! Make good your promise! Your Majesty! I have slain the dragon! Make good your promise!"

The princess laughed when she heard the cries of the steward. How could so pompous, so cowardly a man have killed the dragon? But when he continued to shout and demand his rights, and the dragon's head was brought to town in a cart, she grew fearful and went to her mother and declared that she would rather die than marry the steward.

And so the next morning, with the queen's permission, Iseult, with her maid, Brangien, and her squire, Perenis, set out secretly for the dragon's lair. They found a foreign shield, embossed with the sign of a wild boar. They continued to search and in a nearby cave the princess found a lifeless knight. Fearful that the steward had murdered him, they quickly pulled off his armor and discovered the dragon's tongue lying close to his heart. They brought him back to the castle, and the queen fed him with herbs of theriac until he broke out into a sweat. "He shall soon speak," she said.

Tristan opened his eyes and when he saw the queen, as lovely as the dawn, Iseult, as radiant as the sun, and Brangien, as bright as the full moon, he thought he was in heaven.

"Who are you? And where am I?" he asked.

It was Iseult who spoke first. "Mother, do we not know him? Is he not Tantris, Tantris the minstrel?"

The queen asked, "Are you then the minstrel? Is this your sword? Did you kill the dragon?"

"Yes," the wounded knight said. "Yes. . . ." But before they could ask any more questions, he closed his eyes and fell back asleep.

The queen sent word to the king asking him to delay the steward's request, promising that she would present the true slayer of the dragon in three days' time. Meanwhile, she brewed strong potions and made a healing ointment to remove the venom from the dragon's tongue which had caused the knight to lose his strength.

When he regained some of his strength, Tantris explained to the queen and princess that he had again been robbed and had killed the dragon hoping for recognition, for wherever he traveled he continued to be harried and molested, and he desperately needed protection. They were delighted and in turn asked him to defend the princess against the steward, and he readily agreed.

The princess prepared a bath for the minstrel. As he lay in the bath, she admired his naked body. She gazed at every part of him, even that which he was trying unsuccessfully to hide. All that she saw pleased her, and she thought it unfair that a man of such qualities had not been born of a noble birth so that he would be entitled to honor and to property.

Iseult left him in the bath and went to where his cleaned armor was hidden. She ran her hand lightly across his sword and felt a notch. She stopped. In a daze, she went to her mother's room, opened the iron box and took out the steel splinter. She brought it back, placed it on the stranger's sword. And it fit. It fit exactly!

"Tantris," she mused, "Tan . . . tris—Tris . . . tan. Tristan—Tantris! They are one and the same! It is Tristan who has returned to murder us all!" Her heart grew cold, and with the sword in her hand, Iseult ran into the bath and cried, "Murderer! Traitor! You are Tristan! You killed my uncle, and now I will kill you! You shall die, Tristan!"

"Mercy! Mercy, lady!" he cried. "If you kill me, you will be a murderer! Think of your honor. Do you wish to marry the steward?"

"Murderer!" Iseult shouted again.

On hearing the shouts, the queen entered the room. Weeping, Iseult showed her mother the sword and the splinter. But the queen was slower to anger. She had lived more years, and she had given her word to the king. She led her trembling daughter from the room as the knight cried, "Dear ladies, listen to me, if you would but listen to me, I will give you news to please your hearts."

The queen closed the door and spoke to Iseult. "My child, your anger is mine, and so is your grief. But I would rather bear one grief than two. In all the world there is no one dearer to me than you. Therefore, before we act, let us hear what he has to say." The queen sent for Brangien. Then she sent for the stranger.

The knight entered and fell to the floor before the three women. "Mercy, dear ladies, mercy!" he cried. The queen let him lie there a long time before motioning for him to speak. "Your Majesty, my ladies," he said, "Iseult's words are true. I am Tantris. And I am Tristan." Tears came to the queen's eyes. Lying before her was the very man she had longed to kill; but she preferred her daughter's happiness to her own revenge.

"After you cured me, I returned to Cornwall and sang Iseult's praises to King Mark. But he feared your anger and wished to remain single so I might inherit the throne. I persisted, and at last, he agreed. On Mark's behalf I came to Ireland and risked my life to slay the dragon. Now, if you wish, your daughter may marry a man descended from kings, versed in chivalry, and wealthier even than the king of Ireland." Yes, the queen wished for such a match, and so did the king. Iseult, too, preferred to marry a king rather than a dastardly steward, but she remained angry in her heart with Tristan for deceiving her.

Soon the day arrived for the duel between the steward and the unknown dragon slayer. Tristan sent word with Perenis that the vassals were to come to court in their finest clothes, bringing the holy relics. The court soon filled with Irish barons as well as Cornish knights.

The queen and Iseult entered. The young Iseult shone as radiantly as the sun. On her gold tresses she wore a gold crown of emeralds, jacinth, sapphires, and chalcedony, and over her perfectly fitting purple silk robe, a white ermine mantle trimmed with gray and white sable. Her gait was measured. Her eyes roved the room as freely as a falcon on a bough.

The foolish steward, carrying the dragon's head, approached King Gurmun and said, "Your Majesty, I have come to claim your promise. Here is the dragon's head. Where is the pretender? Let him fight with me!"

The king turned to the queen, and the queen said, "Your Majesty, I will bring him. But first promise me that you will pardon his past deeds, for he risked his life to kill the dragon that has terrified the people of Ireland."

"Grant it, Sire!" the barons cried.

"I grant it," the king said.

Then Perenis brought in Tristan. And when Tristan walked into the hall, the Cornish knights as well as the Irish barons stood up, for no one had ever seen a finer, more distinctive knight than Tristan. He was wearing a gold garment whose silk lining was more purple than violet and quite as purple as iris. It was embroidered with gold and fine pearls; and on his head was a chaplet of chrysolite, topaz, and rubies that glowed like candlelight. He was superb in every detail.

Tristan's knights bowed and placed themselves behind him. Suddenly, one of the Irish barons recognized Tristan and drew his sword and cried, "Is it not Tristan, Tristan of Parmenie, who slew Morholt? Slay him!" And the others raised their swords and cried: "Death to Tristan!" But they soon dropped them, for they remembered the king's promise.

Tristan addressed the assembly, "My lords, I killed Morholt, but I did so in fair combat. Now I have returned to ransom the deed. I have risked my life to rid you of the dragon and to win Iseult for King Mark, who wishes to make her his honored wife and queen of England and Cornwall. As a sign of his wish for friendship between the lands, King Mark has sent you these holy relics."

The court was pleased. They said it was time for peace. War had only brought loss to everyone. It was agreed that England's pages and knights that had been given to Ireland as tribute would be permitted to return to Cornwall with Iseult. Then King Gurmun took Iseult's right hand and put it in Tristan's right hand, asking Tristan to take an oath that he would lead Iseult to her lord. Tristan swore, but Iseult blushed and withdrew her hand.

The noblemen cheered. And then they turned and harassed the pompous steward who had imagined that he could prevail over the greatest of all knights, Tristan of Parmenie.

During the next few days, the queen walked by herself in the countryside, gathering herbs. Her daughter, her only and dearest child, was setting out for an unknown land, and she wanted to protect her.

Careful, my child, your mother loves you so much. How much is so much? How much is too much?

She prepared a love potion from blossoms and grasses, and when it was ready, she called Brangien to her and said, "My child, you will go with your mistress and serve her. I am entrusting you with this flask. Guard it well, for those who drink from it will share one love in their life. This love potion is for King Mark and Iseult. On their wedding night, after they are united, when the king calls for wine, pour the wine from this flask so that they may drink and share one life, one death, one joy, one sorrow."

The king and queen and all the court accompanied Iseult to the harbor. Iseult kissed her mother and father many times. Tristan led Iseult to her cabin and they set sail. But for many days, Iseult refused to leave her cabin. She sulked and wept and feared the new life that was taking her so far from her own land.

One day, when the wind had dropped, Tristan anchored at a small island. Brangien tried to persuade Iseult to go onshore, but she refused. Brangien went with the other vassals onto the island, and Tristan went to Iseult's cabin to try to comfort her.

It was a warm day, and Tristan asked a young serving girl to bring them wine. The young girl, who was a bit lazy, looked about the room and saw on Brangien's bed a small flask of wine half hidden under the covers. She brought the flask to Tristan. He opened it and poured half for Iseult and half for himself. At first, Iseult refused to drink, but as Tristan would not drink until she drank, Iseult drank, and once she began, she drank until she had finished all of her portion. Tristan finished his portion. Then they sat there, staring wordlessly into each other's eyes.

Soon Brangien returned, and when she saw the opened flask and the two staring at each other without speaking, she snatched up the flask and ran and threw it into the sea, weeping and crying, "Too late! Too late!"

What Brangien feared came to be. Tristan and Iseult's hearts opened to each other. At first they tried to avoid each other. Tristan remembered the barons' accusations of his coveting his uncle's land; how much worse to covet his uncle's wife. He remembered how his uncle had made him his heir and had accompanied him to the ship, weeping. Iseult thought of how Tristan had murdered her uncle and torn her from her father and mother and deceived her.

And yet, she loved him. Whatever she thought, wherever she

turned, there was love and there was Tristan. Their eyes sought each other. Their hearts sought each other. They hunted each other. They stalked each other. They contrived to meet.

As the days passed, they did not know where they were or what had happened to them. Brangien knew. She knew and she did not tell.

What is there to tell about love? It is so simple. What you plant is what you sow. But the ground must be well prepared. Yet the ground to which the seed of love fell for Tristan and Iseult could not bear fruit, for the earth they stepped on did not belong to them. It belonged to the king. They did not belong to themselves. They belonged, each of them, to King Mark.

Iseult leaned ever so lightly against Tristan on the deck and sighed, "*Lameir, lameir* pains me so."

"My lady," Tristan said, "is it the tang of the sea that is too strong for you?"

"No, my lord. It is not the sea nor its salt, but love, love that pains me so."

"I, too, my lady. But I am your vassal, not your lord."

"Not so, my lord, for you hold the sword over my heart and my heart belongs to you."

Then they spoke together, as lovers do, of when they had first met and how Tristan had taught her to read and to write and to sing.

Brangien watched as the lovers grew thinner. They were so lost in their desire for each other that they did not think to eat or to drink. After three days, Brangien, fearing for their survival, confessed to them the truth of the contents of the wine they had drank. She begged them to forgive her and to refrain from their passion. But when she saw the anguish each one bore, she agreed to keep their secret and to help them however she could.

That night as Brangien stood guard, Tristan entered Iseult's cabin and the two were joined together. From that night, the journey became for them a voyage of bliss. They were not shy but open and easy and familiar with each other. They held nothing back. They gave of themselves entirely, satisfying each other's every desire. If they had their choice, they would have remained on the sea forever.

When land was sighted, and the others cheered, Tristan and Iseult felt alarm and dread. Fortunately, honor and loyalty rose up in Tristan, enabling him, in all correctness, to present Iseult of the Golden Hair to Mark. And Mark was delighted.

The knights and ladies at court whispered loudly at the sight of Iseult. "What a marvel," they said. "It is true what we have heard of her. Iseult the Fair, Iseult the Blond, is the marvel of the world!"

Eighteen days later, Mark and Iseult were married.

On the night of the wedding, at Iseult's insistence, Brangien took Iseult's place in Mark's bed. Tristan led his uncle to the bedchambers and blew out the candles. Then Brangien slipped into bed and the king drew her to him and was content, for he did not know the difference between brass and gold. As soon as Mark fell asleep, the two women exchanged places. When Mark awoke and called for wine, Brangien poured wine for the king and the queen. Then Mark drew Iseult to him; and again he was content, as content with the gold as with the brass.

Mark adored Iseult. Her dazzling beauty so blinded him that he did not notice, as a husband ought, that she showed him little affection. The people also loved Iseult and spoke of her beauty and talents, her fame and honor. And no one had any suspicion of what took place between the lovers, for since Iseult had been given into Tristan's keeping, it seemed proper that they spend their time together. Thus the lovers were free to enjoy their love.

But one day, Iseult was suddenly overcome with fear. She was afraid that the only one who knew of their love would betray them. Brangien had slept in the king's bed. Would she not prefer to be queen rather than servant?

Iseult summoned two foreign squires and offered them twenty pounds of gold if they would take the girl into the woods and kill her. Then she called Brangien and said that she was not feeling well and needed some herbs for a remedy and that Brangien was to go immediately with the squires.

How cruel, you say. But did I not warn you? Shall I count for you love's ways? Fear, jealousy, revenge—pain. They all belong to love's innocent game.

When they came to a wild place in the forest, the squires drew their swords and told the girl to dismount. In terror Brangien fell to her knees and cried, "In God's name, what will you do?"

"We will kill you," they said, "for it is the queen's command. But first, tell us how you have wronged the queen."

"In God's name, I beg you, I never knowingly did anything to displease the queen. All that I can think of is that when we sailed from Ireland, we each had two shifts as white as snow. On the boat, it was so hot that the queen did not wish to wear anything but her shift. In wearing it night and day the whiteness went out of it. On her wedding day, she did not have a clean shift and asked to borrow mine. I hesitated, but, as she insisted, I agreed. That is all I can think of. If you would kill me, then do so, but tell my lady that I forgive her. Let God protect her and all that she owns. Now do as you wish with me. I give my soul to God."

The squires could not kill the girl. They tied her to a tree and placed her in the high branches so she would be safe from the wolves. Then they cut out the tongue of one of their hunting dogs and brought it back to the queen.

"What did the girl say?" the queen asked.

When the squires repeated Brangien's words, Iseult wept. Then she became inconsolable and cried, "Murderers! Assassins! Brutes! How could you have done such a horrendous deed? I shall kill the two of you for killing my servant!"

"Mercy! Mercy, lady! If you kill us, how will you find the girl?"

"What? She lives? Do not lie! Is my servant alive or dead?"

"She lives. We brought you the tongue of a dog."

"Bring her to me! No, wait. I do not trust you. I will keep one of you as ransom until the other returns."

When Brangien appeared, Iseult rushed to her. She kissed her mouth and cheeks. She kissed her many times, begging her forgiveness. Brangien had passed through Iseult's crucible and from that testing the two remained devoted to each other to the end of their lives.

No, it was not Brangien who betrayed the lovers, but the lovers themselves. After two years, it was not so easy for lovers to conceal their love. Countless times during the day their eyes sought each other with tender glances. They disappeared into the queen's chambers and did not reappear for hours. But it was not until the incident with the Irish baron that suspicion was aroused.

One day, when Tristan was away hunting, a tall, manly baron appeared at court wearing over his shoulder a lavishly decorated lyre. Gandin had often escorted Iseult in Ireland, and it was on her account that he had come to Cornwall. To please Iseult, Mark treated the queen's former countryman with courtesy and invited him to dine with them. Gandin sat beside Mark and ate and drank, and when the board was removed, Mark invited Gandin to play a song for the court on his lyre. The arrogant Gandin refused to play without a reward. Impetuously, Mark opened his arms wide and replied, "I am at your service. Play for us and I will give you whatever you wish."

Gandin played two songs for the court and then said, "I claim Iseult, who is fairer than gold."

"Do not be foolish," the king said lightly.

But Gandin became indignant and cried. "Your Majesty, where is your honor? If you do not keep your word, you are not fit to be king! I am willing to risk my life. I claim Iseult. Whoever contests my claim, let him fight with me."

The king looked up at the tall, stalwart baron, and as no other vassal came forward, Gandin quickly left the court with the weeping Iseult.

How generous the king is. Why, the world is filled with such generous, courteous men of their word. Wouldn't a wife prefer the rude man?

When Tristan returned and found that the queen had been taken away, he took his harp and rode at once to the landing place. Tying his horse at a distance, he approached Gandin, who was sitting with the queen in a silken tent, waiting for the tide to come in.

"Noble baron," Tristan said, "I have been told that you are returning to Dublin. I am a harper from Ireland and long to be reunited with my land. I beg you, take me home with you."

"You have my word. But first, play for us. Can you not see the lady is weeping?"

The harper played. Iseult stopped weeping. And the tide drifted in. Gandin's men called from the ship urging them to come aboard before Tristan and trouble should arrive. But Gandin ignored them and asked the minstrel to play "Dido's Song." Soon the water rose to such a height that a long-legged horse was needed to reach the ship's gangplank. Tristan offered his horse. Gandin offered him fine clothes in exchange.

When Tristan returned with his horse, Iseult refused to go to the boat unless the minstrel carried her. Gandin was thus forced to carefully hand his lady to Tristan, who set Iseult in front of him and galloped off in the opposite direction.

"Stop, fool!" Gandin shouted.

"Fool?" Tristan repeated. "You confuse us. You outwitted the king. But Tristan has outwitted you. Keep your fine clothes, my cuckoo. You have given me the best your tent has to offer."

Tristan and Iseult did not return to court until late that evening. Then Tristan, looking pointedly at the barons, advised the king to be more cautious about giving away the queen for a song.

Soon after this, two barons discovered Tristan and Iseult naked in Mark's bed. They conferred with the other barons and then went to Mark and spoke harshly. "Sire, you have placed your trust in Tristan, and Tristan has deceived you. Tristan loves the queen! And the queen loves Tristan!"

"Villains! Cowards!!" the king cried. "How dare you speak evil against Tristan? Twice he risked his life to save yours!"

"Sire, it is a known fact, and we are not the only ones who speak of it. If you do not banish your nephew, we will leave your court and take the other barons with us. We cannot live at court with such dishonor."

Mark was silent. Tristan was his delight; Iseult his joy. But he knew he could not remain king without his barons. Mark was forced to choose.

But what to choose, and whom to choose, and when to choose, and how to choose? And how to win and not to lose? Or how to win and not to choose? Ah!

"Advise me," Mark said. "You are my counselors. I do not know how my nephew could have wished to have shamed me. But I do not want to lose your service. What shall I do?"

"Send for the prophetic dwarf, Frocin," the barons said. "He will devise a plan."

Mark sent for Frocin. Frocin arrived and advised Mark to send Tristan before dawn with a sealed letter to King Arthur, but not to tell Tristan of his mission until they had retired to the bedroom. The dwarf predicted that Tristan would not be able to resist visiting the queen before he left in the morning.

After Tristan received his mission, he lay in his bed and could not sleep. He heard footsteps and watched as the malicious dwarf crept into the room and sprinkled flour on the floor between the king's bed and Tristan's bed. Tristan knew it would be folly for him to visit the queen that night, but as soon as the others went out of the room, his passion overcame his good sense, and he leapt from his bed to the king's. There were no footprints, but that day Tristan had been hurt during the hunt, and as he leapt, his wound opened and bled. Outside the palace, Frocin looked at the full moon and said, "Now, let us go in. They are lying together."

Tristan heard them enter and leapt back to his bed and pretended to be asleep. But by the light of the candles, the barons followed the track of bright red blood from the king's bed to Tristan's bed. They threw the covers off Tristan's bed and when they saw his bleeding leg, they held him fast and cried, "Vengeance, your Majesty! Take vengeance!"

The anguished king cried, "You shall die, Tristan! You and the queen shall be burned by fire!"

"The queen has done no wrong!" Tristan cried. "Sire, in the name of Christ, do not harm the queen. If any man would accuse the queen of acting sinfully let him fight with me!"

The king would not listen. Tristan was dragged away by the guards.

In the morning, at the first hour, the king ordered a ditch to be dug, which was to be covered with vines and thorns. The people gathered outside the palace begging the king to show mercy on Tristan, their defender. In his anger the king said,

"Whoever petitions me shall be burnt first!" When the barons petitioned Mark for a trial, he said, "Light the fire!"

The guards led Tristan toward the plain where a large crowd was already assembled around the fire. On the way they passed a small stone chapel on a high cliff overlooking the sea. Tristan said to his guards, "I beg you, my death has come. Let me say my last prayer in peace and ask Christ to forgive me."

As there was only one door, the guards let him enter the chapel. But the moment he was inside, Tristan bolted the door, broke the window, and leapt, preferring to die rather than to be shamed before the people. God was with Tristan, and the wind caught his cloak and carried him away from the cliff, dropping him into the sea.

Tristan swam for shore. When he reached the land, he saw in one direction smoke and crackling flames. He ran in the other direction, and there riding toward him, to his joy and relief, was his faithful servant Govenal, who, fearful of the king's wrath, had fled the palace, taking with him Tristan's sword and charger.

"Quickly, Govenal!" Tristan shouted. "God has saved my life, but if I do not save the queen, I would sooner be dead!"

"Slow-ly—slow-ly," Govenal counseled. "Let us ride to the fire, hide near the thicket, and wait for our revenge."

At this moment, the queen was being led through the streets to the fire. Her long golden hair fell to her waist. Her head was bowed. Her hands were bound. She wore a plain gray linen shift. Tears streamed down her cheeks. The people watched their once glorious queen and wept. Even the envious barons wept. Again they pleaded with the king for a fair trial. But the artless king, who had been blind with passion, was now blind with rage.

As Iseult approached the fire, the leper Ivain, followed by a crowd of lepers, went up to the king and cried, "Sire, your justice is harsh but it is short. It will not last. The fire will burn her and in moments she will be ashes. But if you let me speak, I can tell you of a way in which her pain will go on forever."

"Speak, leper. What is your way?" the king asked. "If you know of a grimmer death, I will reward you."

"Give her to me!" Ivain cried, "Give her to me and to all my comrades! We will enjoy her together. There's enough lust in us to cripple her in a day. With you she lived in a castle and wore fine clothes and ate fine food. With us she'll live in a hovel and eat crumbs. In our courts she'll rather be dead than alive!"

"Mercy! Mercy, Your Majesty," Iseult pleaded. "Let me rather be burned by fire!" The blind king took her arm and gave her to Ivain.

How unkind. But he is blind. Blind, blind, blind. Pity the wife who is wed. Pity the people who are led by the king, who is blind, blind, blind. . . .

A cry went up from the other lepers. With their open sores oozing, they hobbled on their crutches, reaching for the queen. Ivain pushed them away and started toward the open road with his prize when out of the bushes rode Tristan and Govenal. Tristan lifted Iseult up onto his horse; Govenal swung his sword in all directions, toppling the beggars; and in moments, the two horses disappeared into the woods. Mark offered a reward of one hundred silver pounds to anyone who would bring back Tristan. No one dared.

The king burned with anger. But after several months, when he looked about his court, nowhere did he see a knight to compare to Tristan in valor, in merit, or in eagerness. Mark longed for Tristan. He languished for Iseult.

The lovers fled. They fled over rocks and brambles. They fled through the forest until, after many days, they came to the Woods of Morois. Govenal returned to Cornwall. Under a leafy lime tree, the lovers built a hut of leaves and branches over a carpet of green grass. There was sunshine. There was shade. There were flowering fruit trees, bushes, flowing streams, the song of the nightingale, the song of the thrush. There was Man. There was Woman.

Some say other pastimes are needed. But I remember, long ago, a time when love alone was sufficient. Shall I count for you love's ways? Pleasure, tenderness, passion—ecstasy. These are the ways of love's innocent game.

When winter came and there was little to eat, they were still content. They found a cave and told each other love stories and sang and played the harp in turn. They loved each other as their hearts prompted. How did they love? Their love was a part of the cave, and the cave was round and high and broad. As their bodies weakened, for there was little food, their love soared, filling the expanse of the cave, exploring the depths of their hearts. In the roundness of the cave, they came to know the tender curves of love's inner circles.

And there was more! But I cannot tell it, for I do not know it. It belongs only to the lovers.

Winter passed and spring came. The blackbird, the thrush and the nightingale sang. Tristan imitated bird calls. Then, one day, they heard the king and his party hunting in the woods nearby, and they were afraid. That night Tristan placed a sword between them; and it happened that at dawn a huntsman chasing a white runaway hart discovered the lover's cave and led the king to the cave, hoping for a reward.

Mark approached the cave ready to kill the lovers, but when he saw the naked sword separating Tristan and Iseult, he did not know if they were innocent or guilty. He looked at the two he loved the most in the world. Iseult had never looked so beautiful.

She wore on her head not a crown but a chaplet of clover. Her cheeks were flushed. Her throat was white. Her breasts were round and full. Mark looked at Tristan. Tristan's lips were parted as if in song. Mark remembered the many songs Tristan had sung for him when he was a young man at court.

At that moment, a tiny sunbeam entered the cave and danced across Iseult's red lips. Mark chose to see what he wished to see. He knelt and placed his glove by the queen's cheek. Then he took Tristan's sword and replaced it with his own and quietly left the cave.

A moment later, Iseult woke with a start. She had dreamt that two lions were about to devour her. She begged for mercy, but they were so hungry they began to eat her hands. She screamed. Tristan woke and reached for his sword. But it was not his sword. It was the king's sword. Then Iseult saw the king's glove.

"We must flee!" Tristan said. "The king has discovered us. We must flee!"

They fled. They fled toward Wales. They fled, not daring to spend the night where they spent the day. They wandered in the forest like wild animals until a change came over them. . . .

I told you of the love potion which the queen had made. Yes, but I did not tell you of its duration. A story takes a moment or two to unravel, and certain details are best left till later—which is to say now.

If those who drank the love potion were separated before four years' time, they would die of anguish. But after four years, although their hearts would remain as one, they would not be ruled by the potion and could live apart. Four years. Four seasons. Four directions. Turn!

And so it happened that after four years, at a certain hour, Tristan was in the woods hunting, and he stopped. He thought of the king and how he had wronged him. He had estranged Mark from his wife. The king had not known of the love potion they had drunk, and yet, when he had discovered them in the cave, he had been merciful. He thought of Iseult and how he had wronged her. She had been given into his keeping. She was the daughter of the king of Ireland and deserved to live in a palace with servants and fine clothes, not to be wandering in the woods like a hunted animal—

At the same hour, Iseult thought of the king. From the moment she had arrived in Cornwall, he had treated her with honor and respect. The man who had given her over to the leper was not the same king as the one who had given her his glove. And Tristan—Tristan was the greatest of knights! He should be leading vassals to war, hunting and hawking and gaining great merit.

And so when Tristan returned, they spoke together and decided to go to Friar Ogrin, who lived in the woods, to ask his help in bringing about a reconciliation with the king. On the lovers' behalf the friar wrote a letter to the king.

They turned! The lovers turned. But to what did they turn? Honor? Merit? Mark? What do you say? Speak up. By now, you know as much as I do.

Friar Ogrin wrote to Mark asking him to take back Tristan and Iseult. If the king would not accept Tristan as his knight, then Tristan would cross the seas to serve other kings. But if the king would not accept Iseult as his wife, then Tristan, who had been given Iseult into his keeping, would bring her back to Ireland where she might reign as queen.

They soon received a reply stating that Mark welcomed back Iseult. But the court refused to allow Tristan to remain in Cornwall. Three days after Iseult returned to Tintagel, Tristan was to cross the seas to serve other kings.

The lovers went into the woods for the last time. They followed a stream and sat by a pine tree and spoke. Iseult held Tristan's hand and said, "For so long now my heart has been yours, wherever you go, my heart will still be yours. But promise me you will guard your life well; for if you die, I will not live. And I will guard my life, not for my sake, but for yours. We are one life, one flesh, one Tristan, one Iseult."

Tristan said. "No matter what happens to my heart, you will never leave it."

Then Iseult took from her finger a green ring and gave it to Tristan and said, "As my life is yours, this ring is yours. If you are ever drawn to love another woman, remember this moment and how my heart feels; and let no one be closer to your heart than Iseult. And if you ever need me, send me this ring, and no king or wall or tower will keep me from you. Oh, kiss me, my friend, kiss me, and let our kiss be a pledge that we remain one Tristan, one Iseult, undivided."

Iseult prepared to return to Cornwall, but Tristan, at Iseult's request, did not leave at once. He secretly stayed in the forest with the forester, for Iseult feared the envy of the barons.

Friar Ogrin went to buy clothes for Iseult. With great pleasure, he spent his life's savings on lavish silks and wools as well as a gentle palfrey which had a saddle with gold trimmings.

On the day the queen returned to Tintagel, the streets were strewn with flowers, the bells tolled, and great silks and tapestries hung from every window. Not since the day of their wedding had the queen been so honored. Mark, too, was happy. Although he did not share with Iseult the glorious things that God can bring to pass between lovers, he was happy, for he possessed the queen in body as well as in name.

But as Iseult feared, so it came to be. A month after her return, when the barons were hunting with the king, they said, "Sire, the queen has returned. But she has not vindicated herself. If she can not prove her innocence, she must be banished."

"By God, will you never be done? First you have driven away my nephew. Now you would banish my wife. When Tristan offered to defend her, all of you were silent."

Still, when the king returned home, he was troubled. Iseult spoke softly but firmly. "Your Majesty, I am willing to make my defense, but I am afraid that no matter how many trials I undergo your barons will ask for more. Therefore, ask King Arthur and his household to be my witness this one time and for all time."

The king agreed. Word was sent to Stirling to request King Arthur's presence. And Iseult sent her squire, Perenis, to ask Tristan to be at the shore by the White Land, dressed as a miserable pilgrim, ten days after the new moon.

The members of King Mark's court as well as King Arthur's court waited in great numbers at the White Land. No one recognized Tristan, for he had stained his face yellow and blackened his clothes. He was wearing a ragged cloak and leaning on a gnarled staff.

When Iseult arrived by boat from Cornwall, she asked that the hearty pilgrim by the shore carry her through the marshy land to the plain. The pilgrim was summoned, and as he held Iseult in his arms, she whispered in his ear, "As soon as we reach land, stumble and fall between my legs." Tristan did as she asked. He put her down and fell into her lap. The attendants pulled him away and were about to beat him, but the queen said, "let him be, he has done his best."

A gray silk cloth was spread over the grass. The holy relics on which the queen was to swear her oath were taken out of the minster and placed on the silk cloth. The barons paced up and down, debating the exact wording of the oath Iseult was to take. But before they reached their decision, the queen stood and spoke, "My kings, my lords, I take my oath: I swear to you by God, and by these holy relics, that no man ever came between my thighs but my king, and this poor pilgrim who carried me from the boat and fell on me in the sight of all of you."

Then King Arthur said, "Let the queen be given the iron."

Iseult took the iron, carried it, and then put it down. Her hands were without blemish.

King Arthur said, "We have witnessed the queen's innocence and accept her defense. If she is ever troubled again, as soon as she sends word, we will defend her. Mark, remain steadfast, and do not trust the villains who would speak ill of your queen. She has given her oath." The two kings then returned to their courts.

Ah, these kings. What do they tell each other? Be content. Trust your wife. I say better to heed the ways of a fool. Merry one day, miserable the next. Trust no one—but the fool.

Several days later, Tristan set sail. Iseult watched Tristan's ship sail and felt her soul was leaving her. Where shall I find myself now? she wondered. Tristan departs and leaves with my life, I am here, sitting at Mark's side. I am there, sailing with Tristan. And I am nowhere. Whoever was so divided? Tristan must leave if he would live. Anyone who would stop his friend from living is no friend. But how can *I* live? How can I live in such torment? How is it that my heart does not break? Oh Tristan, no two lives were ever so intermingled. We hold each other's death and life. I must live so you may live. Live, my friend."

Tristan sailed to Wales, where he stayed with the carefree Duke Gilan. The duke owned a marvel—a wondrous fairy dog named Petit-Cru. When Tristan saw this beautiful little fairy dog, he wanted it for Iseult. He made a wager with the duke, won it, and had a Welsh minstrel deliver the fairy dog to Iseult, hoping it would assuage her sorrow.

From the moment Iseult held Petit-Cru in her arms, she was happy. She stroked its soft, silky fur. She held it to the light. Its fur changed from moment to moment, taking on every color in the rainbow: azure, saffron, clover, scarlet, black, white, violet.

Iseult was content. It was only after a week that she realized that there was a magical spell attached to the bell which hung around the dog's gold collar. The tinkling sound of the crystal bell caused its listeners to fall into a trance, forgetting all grief or sorrow. At this discovery, Iseult pulled the bell off the dog's collar and threw it into the sea. How can I live in happiness, she said, while Tristan is in distress? If my life is his, I will share his sorrow as well as his joy. And so she gave up her chance for pleasure.

From Wales Tristan sailed to Parmenie. His parents were dead, but his brothers welcomed him warmly. They took him stalking and hunting. They visited knights and ladies. They attended tournaments. But Tristan remained in anguish. To rid himself of his agony, he set off for the wars in Germany. He won great merit in Germany and then went on to Spain. After two years, he returned to Parmenie. In all of this time, he had had no word from Iseult. His life was a living death without his lady.

Near Parmenie was the small duchy of Arundel. At this time, the Count of Nantes was attacking the duke, for he wished to carry off the duke's daughter. Hoping to forget his sorrow, Tristan rode to Arundel. Soon he and the duke's son, Kaherdin, became companions, and together they routed the count from Arundel.

Kaherdin then brought Tristan to meet his sister. The name of the sister of Kaherdin was also Iseult, Iseult of the Fair Hands. When Tristan heard her name and saw how lovely she was, his old pain returned. Yet, he was glad of this pain, for it brought him closer to his lady. Tristan spent many days with Kaherdin and his sister. When he looked at Iseult of the Fair Hands, he thought of his own Iseult, and he composed many beautiful melodies which he sang for the two Iseults. There was one refrain which he sang again and again:

Iseult, my fair, Iseult, my breath,
Iseult, my life, Iseult, my death.

He sighed so as he sang that those who listened thought he was sighing for love of Iseult of the Fair Hands. Iseult, too, thought he was languishing for her, and she sighed when he sighed. She laughed when he laughed. She turned shining eyes toward him and made herself so alluring that Tristan was caught by her affections.

When Tristan was alone he spoke to his lady, first blaming himself, then blaming her. "My lady, how faithless I have been. You have kept your pledge. You love only one Tristan. I love two Iseults. But I am far from you, and I have no joy in life. If you loved me, you would have sent a messenger who would have searched the world until he found me. But you have your fairy dog and delight in Mark, who takes his pleasure in your body, whereas I, I have given up all pleasure for your sake. Perhaps if I were to divert my passion, I might know what it is that you experience with Mark. I, too, want pleasure. I, too, wish to live."

In his confusion, Tristan imagined, as many of us do, that in going against love he could gain love. Tristan allowed his grief to turn to anger—not so difficult—for as we have seen, he was already drawn to another woman.

And so when Kaherdin asked him his intentions regarding his sister, Tristan said that he wished to marry her, and the wedding was soon arranged.

On Tristan's wedding night, his valet drew off Tristan's tunic and the green ring fell to the floor. As Tristan knelt to pick it up, he remembered the day in the forest when Iseult had given it to him. He remembered the Woods of Morois, and how she had suffered for him, and how she had loved him. He remembered their kiss and their pledge.

His heart spoke to him. And he understood that although whatever he would do he would hurt one of the Iseults, he knew he must obey his heart. His wife was waiting. Tristan sat down on the bed. What was to have been a great pleasure was now a duty he could not complete. His wife opened her arms and said, "My love—"

"My friend," he said, "I am sorry. An old wound has reawoken on my left side. We must wait for another time to take our pleasure."

"Oh, my lord," she said, "I am more sorry for this wound than for any other ill in the world. But I will wait until you are well."

The next day, when they placed the wimple of the married woman on her head, Iseult of the Fair Hands did not speak of what had happened on her wedding night. But a month later when she and her brother were riding though the stream and her horse stumbled and the water splashed her thighs, she laughed so loudly that her brother asked, "Sister, why do you laugh in this way?"

"Brother," she answered, "this water is more bold than ever was bold the bold lord Tristan." On further questioning, she told her brother the truth of her marriage.

Kaherdin angrily confronted Tristan, and Tristan said, "Come, my friend, ride with me into the woods and I will tell you my misery." In the forest, Tristan revealed the story of his heart to his friend. Kaherdin listened in amazement and sadness. Then he said, "This is my advice. Let us go to Cornwall and see if your lady still cares for you. If she has forgotten you, then perhaps you can give yourself freely to my sister."

Tristan said, "The heart of a friend is worth more than all the gold in a country's treasury. Let us go, my friend."

Tristan and Kaherdin sailed for Cornwall disguised as pilgrims. On the day they arrived, Mark's court was returning to Tintagel. They hid behind bushes and watched the procession. First came the king's procession, then the queen's. In the queen's procession, the serving girls rode first, then the wives of the nobles and barons; and finally, there rode the loveliest woman Kaherdin had ever seen. "Is it, the queen?" Kaherdin whispered to Tristan. "Is it, Iseult?"

"No," Tristan replied, "that is her attendant, Brangien. Wait." At that moment, the road grew bright, as bright as if a cloud had suddenly moved away from the sun, and there appeared the most beautiful woman in all of England and Cornwall, Iseult the Fair, Iseult of the Golden Hair.

That night as Iseult lay sleepless in the king's arms, she listened to a nightingale singing. It seemed to be lamenting rather than singing. She thought of Tristan and of the Woods of Morois and how he had imitated the songs of the birds. Just then the melody quivered, and she knew it was Tristan. She slipped from the bed, out of the room, down the stairs, through the corridors, into the garden, and stopped. Standing against the wall was Tristan. Her heart leapt. Her face burned. In a moment she was in his arms laughing and weeping without a sound. They held each other all night.

The next morning the king left for six days to hold court at St. Lubin's, and the lovers lived in bliss. On the day Mark was to return, Iseult pleaded with Tristan, "Flee, my lord, flee, so you may live."

"And how can I live?" Tristan asked.

"Live so I may live. And if you need me, send me the ring, and no king or wall or tower will keep me from you."

Tristan found Kaherdin and together they returned to Arundel.

When Mark came back to Tintagel and heard that Tristan had dared to deceive him again, he regretted that he had ever spared Tristan. He sent word to Parmenie that Tristan had forfeited his right to return to Cornwall. He tripled the ransom on Tristan's life.

Tristan was then in great distress. How can I live without my lady? he thought. And my lady? Will she imagine I am too cowardly to risk seeing her? No, there is always a way, even a fool . . . And then, Tristan knew what he would do.

Ah, friends, pay close attention, for Tristan has caught on! Tristan would take my place!

He shaved his hair. He scratched his face. He ate herbs so that his cheeks puffed up. He set out without horse or sword or helmet. He walked. He suffered and he walked.

He crossed the seas and changed his name and his voice. He brandished his stick and swatted at all who crossed his path. He entered the castle at Tintagel and no one dared to stop him, for he had become a fool!

He went up to the king and queen and bowed.

"Fool," said the king, "what is your name?"

"Peecus, your Majesty."

"And who is your father?"

"A walrus."

"And your mother?"

"A whale. Your Majesty, give me your wife to wed, and I will give you my sister in exchange."

"And what will you do with my wife?"

"I will build for us a house of flowers and roses in the sky, and there we will be merry. But, your Majesty, you know I have another name. Tantris. I am Tantris the minstrel. Ask Brangien. She knows. She remembers the love potion that caused us all such distress. And if she says it's a lie, then it's a lie that I have dreamt every night since."

"Enough jesting, Picolay," said the king.

"Too much sorrow and too little jest. On guard, your Majesty! Look at me! You remember the naked sword in the Woods of Morois?"

"Fool!" cried the queen, "You should have drowned in the waters in which you were born."

"Oh, my lady, have you forgotten me, too? If you remembered me, then no king or wall or tower would keep you from me. I have suffered greatly because of you. Oh kiss me, my lady, kiss me this instant. Lift up your skirts and make up for all the kisses I have lost. How I have missed your sweet kisses under the sheets!"

"Enough jesting!" cried the king, and he called for his horse and left the hall to watch the cranes fly. But Iseult went to her room and said to Brangien, "The fool mocks me; and yet, I would speak to him. Bring him to me."

Tristan entered the queen's room. He bowed politely and said, "My lady, I am a lover and I am a madman. But if you knew me, I would no longer be mad. Look at me! Do you not know the minstrel who taught you to write and to sing in your castle? Do you not know the young knight who drank the love potion with you in your cabin? Do you not know your lover who shared your bed in the Woods of Morois? Do you not know the fool?"

"I know," said Iseult, "that someone has taught you well, but you in no way resemble the noble knight Tristan."

"Ah, my lady, once I had a love; but now, I have none. I have such sorrow."

"And who has caused you such sorrow?"

"My lady who caused me such joy. Yet I have one hope left—her pledge. When we parted, she gave me her pledge. It is a small token, but it has never left my person. Perhaps she will recognize it?" Then he took from his pouch a green ring. When Iseult saw it, she knew at once it was Tristan and she fainted. Tristan caught her.

Soon she opened her eyes and said, "Oh, my love, forgive me. I am the fool. How did my heart not know the man who has endured such suffering for me? Oh, come my lord, come and forgive me in all sweetness." Then Iseult led him to her bed and gave him the joy and comfort that he had been waiting for for so long.

But the next day when the fool tried to enter the queen's bedroom, one of the queen's servants was guarding the door. Tristan pushed him aside and went into Iseult's room. "My friend, they suspect that I am here. I must flee . . ."

"Tristan, hold me. Hold me until our hearts break and we fly together to the house of flowers and roses in the sky. Tristan, take me with you!"

"My love, if I send for you, will you come?"

"You know I will."

Tristan opened the door. The guards tried to stop him, but he swung his fool's stick at them and said, "Easy, champions, I will not stay. I am on my way to prepare the house of flowers and roses that I have promised my lady."

Tristan returned to Arundel. He was separated once again from Iseult but not from love. By now, Tristan was known throughout Brittany and Normandy for his compassion for those who suffered in love, and many came to Tristan for help.

One day, a knight, a dwarf whose name was also Tristan, pleaded with Tristan to help him rescue his wife who had been stolen by Estult and his six fierce brothers. Tristan and the knight set out through the woods for Estult's castle. On the way, the six brothers attacked them. The fight began and did not end until all were dead except Tristan.

With great difficulty, Tristan made his way back to Arundel. The doctors were summoned and dressed his wounds, but they could not cure him. Tristan lost weight. His bones showed through his skin. He was tormented by the pain and the stench. At last, one day he called for Kaherdin and sent everyone from his room. Iseult of the Fair Hands, fearing that her husband intended to become a monk, listened behind the wall in the next room as her husband spoke.

"Kaherdin, I am dying and the only one who can cure me is the queen of Cornwall. She learned the healing from her mother long ago in Ireland. I beg you, go to her, give her this green ring, and bid her by the love potion we drank, by our pledge, and by the joys and sorrows we have shared that she come to me quickly and not fail me."

"I will leave at once." Kaherdin said. "I will tell no one what you have said, only that I am going in search of a woman healer."

"Then go, my friend, and take my ship. If you bring the queen back, as you enter the harbor raise the white sails. I will be waiting. But if she will not come, so that I can prepare myself, then raise the black ones."

Iseult of the Fair Hands, who had heard every word her husband had spoken, then understood why her husband's joy had been lost to her. It had belonged to another woman. She hid her anger in her heart and went into her husband, showing him all affection and concern.

In the guise of a merchant, Kaherdin sailed for Cornwall. In twenty days he reached Tintagel and went to the court with boxes of rare cloth, precious gold, and fine jewelry. He showed the queen a beautiful gold clasp, and as she was admiring it, he took from his pouch a green ring and said quietly, "Perhaps Your Majesty would prefer this ring?"

The queen at once motioned for Kaherdin to follow her, and when they were far from the others, she said, "Speak to me of this ring."

"My Lady, Tristan is dying. He has been wounded by a poisoned spear and no one can cure him. He begs you by this ring, and by your pledge, and by all you have lived and suffered together to return with me to heal him, for he can not hold on much longer."

Iseult consulted Brangien. Then she returned to Kaherdin and said, "We will meet you this evening at your ship."

Under cover of darkness, Iseult and Brangien stole quietly out of the palace and went down to the harbor. The wind was strong and the ship sailed swiftly. But just as they were in sight of land, a storm came up, a tempest so strong that all who were on board wept and cried in fear. The sails were lowered, and for five days the tempest raged and the ship turned round and round. Iseult begged God to allow her to reach Tristan in time.

At last, the wind dropped and the storm ended. Kaherdin hoisted the white sails and entered the harbor. But Tristan had become so weak he had to return to his room and ask his wife to sit by the harbor and wait for the ship. When Iseult of the Fair Hands saw the ship, she hastened to Tristan's room.

Tristan, take my fool's stick. Tell your wife your story. Beg her forgiveness. Speak, my eloquent Tristan, speak! What is it? A cruel surfeit of courtesy? A fatal lack of courage? There is little time. Off with the mask! Speak! But you are too weak— the game, love's game, is played. . . .

"My lord," she said, "my brother has returned. This very moment your ship has entered the harbor."

"Beautiful lady," Tristan said, "tell me, beautiful lady, what color are the sails?"

"The sails are plain to see, for there is little wind and he has hoisted them high. The sails, my lord, are black."

At these words, Tristan felt more pain than he had ever felt in his life. He turned his face to the wall and said, "My love, you could not come to me, and I can not hold on any longer." He spoke her name four times, "Iseult . . . Iseult . . . Iseult . . . Iseult." And he died.

Iseult of the Fair Hands fell to the floor, weeping. The news of Tristan's death passed through the great house, and the knights and ladies wept loudly.

At that moment the ship docked. As Iseult and Brangien went onto the shore, they heard the bells tolling and the people weeping. Iseult asked an old man what had happened. "Oh, my lady," he said, "it is a great sorrow, a great sorrow. The best knight, the noblest who ever lived, Tristan of Parmenie, is dead."

Iseult could scarcely breathe. She threw off her cloak and hurried through the streets toward the castle. The Bretons who saw her pass marveled at the sight of her, for they had never seen a woman of such dazzling beauty.

Iseult entered Tristan's room and said to the kneeling woman, "Rise, my lady, and let me near him. I have more right to mourn him than you, for we have loved each other all these years."

Then she lay down beside him and took him in her arms. She kissed his eyes, his cheeks, his mouth. And then she held him. She held him. Until her soul joined his.One man, one woman, one woman, one man. Tristan, Iseult, Iseult, Tristan. Round and round. Up and down. The masks are off. My fool's tale is done.

GLOSSARY

Abzu (Sumerian: 𒍪 𒀊 abyss, sea, home of Enki) The shrine of Enki, the god of wisdom; a banquet hall in Enki's sea home, where no light penetrates. It is located in Eridu near the reed marshes by the Persian Gulf. The *me* are stored in the Abzu. In Sumerian myth, Enki's city and shrine are described as pure places made of lapis and silver, filled with the music of sacred songs and spells. *See Me,* Eridu.

An (Sumerian: 𒀭 𒀭 heaven) Sky god, father of gods. His consorts include Ki and Urash (goddesses of the earth) and Nammu (goddess of the watery deep). He is represented as a bull; his voice is the thunder; his semen is the rain. An determines the destinies of the gods and mortals. The Sumerian primordial flood was attributed to An and Enlil's anger.

Ankh (Egyptian: ☥| life) A small crosslike symbol representing the breath of life. The upper portion is a loop and points to the divine. On the wall paintings in the tombs, the gods often offer the ankh to the nose of the king, thus giving him the breath of life.

Anubis (Egyptian: dog) The god of the dead. He guards the mummy from evil forces. He appears as a dog-jackal. In the afterlife, in the presence of Osiris, Anubis conducts the weighing of the heart in the Hall of Judgement and is responsible for the revivification of the dead. *See* Thoth, Osiris.

Anzu (Sumerian:) A great legendary bird who is depicted as a lion-headed eagle. In the Akkadian myth, Anzu steals the tablets of destiny from Enlil, halting the world order. The gods are afraid to pursue him; only the hero Ninurta dares and is helped by the advice of Enki-Ea. The birth of Anzu is mysteriously connected to a change in the nature of the earth's waters.

Apopis (Egyptian: snake) Serpent of darkness. Each morning and evening, Apopis attacks the Sunboat, trying to prevent the rebirth of the sun, thus threatening the existence of the world.

Arali (Sumerian:) A name for the underworld.

Atum (Egyptian:) The creator god who is the invisible manifestation of the sun god. He journeys through the underworld each night. Atum first took shape in the Nun as a snake. His epithets include the Complete One, Lord of All, Great Serpent.

Baba/Bebon (Egyptian: or) Protective god. Highly sexual. His negative character is associated with Seth.

Bacchus (Greek: Βάκχος) or Dionysus (Greek: Διόνυσος) God of wine. In Greek myth, the son of Zeus and Semele is snatched from the womb of his dying mother by Zeus, who then gives birth to him from his thigh. Dionysus appears with his flowing hair crowned with horns and ivy leaves, holding a thyrsus in his hand. Struck mad by the jealous Hera, he is cured when initiated into the rites of Semele. He discovers the culture of wine and initiates frenzied rites of joy and sorrow for women.

Bath-Rabbim (Hebrew: בת רבים daughter of many, possibly helper of the Canaanite deity, Rbm [a Sea God]). Used to designate the city of Heshbon or possibly its gates.

Belili An ancient goddess, who is mentioned with Geshtinanna as the sister of Dumuzi.

Brahma (Sanskrit: ब्रह्मा large) In the trinity of gods, the four-faced Creator was born from a golden thousand-petaled lotus, which was attached to sleeping Vishnu's navel. He appears with red skin, wearing white robes, riding on a white Hamsa, a swan or goose. In his four hands, he holds the Vedas, which are said to have sprung from his head, a water jug, and Parivita, his bow. Saraswati, created from Brahma's mind, tried to flee from him. When she fled into the air, Brahma grew a fifth head to find her and joined with her, making her his wife. Shiva later deprived Brahma of his fifth head. Brahma is associated with the heart (consciousness), the root of a tree, and the world-egg. He is the source of action, motion, rhythms, forms, thoughts.

Ceres (Latin) or Demeter (Greek: Δημήτηρ) Goddess of the harvest, fertility, corn, and grain. Her consort is Jupiter. She wears a garland of corn in her golden hair and carries a sickle in her right hand and a torch in her left hand. Coiled dragons lie at her feet as well as the cornucopia. In Greek myth, she searched the earth for her lost daughter, Persephone, and her grief caused famine on earth. Zeus prevailed on Hades to release Persephone and spring came back to the earth. *See* Eleusis.

Charon (Greek: Χάρων bright, fierce) God of the underworld. Son of Pluto according to Apuleius. Other traditions claim he is the son of Erebus (darkness) and Nyx (night). Charon conducts the shades in his ferry-boat across the River Styx to the House of Hades. No one can cross without tribute.

Cnidos (Greek: κνίδος) A Greek port in Asia Minor where there was an important temple to Venus.

Cythera (Greek: Κύθηρα) An island off the coast of the Peloponnesus where an important cult center of Aphrodite was located. The name, Cythereia, became an epithet for Aphrodite. According to some Greek traditions, after floating in the sea, Aphrodite was washed ashore on Cythera.

Daksha (Sanskrit: दक्ष intelligent, nimble with one's hands) Ritual-Skill. The first Daksha was born from Brahma's right thumb. His consort was Prasuti. At Brahma's orders, the second Daksha, together with his wife, the Dark-One, who is the daughter of Virani, created all living beings. Shiva sacrificed Daksha's head in the fire; but then persuaded by the other gods, Shiva allowed Daksha to live again with the head of a goat. Daksha became an expert in rituals, respected by gods and mortals. The quarrel between Daksha (Brahma's son) and Shiva is a continuation of the rivalry between Shiva and Brahma for supremacy.

David (Hebrew: דוד beloved of God) A king of Israel in the tenth century B.C.E. Son of Jesse and Nazbat. He had many wives; his chief wife was Bathsheba. He began his career at King Saul's court playing the lyre. Later, he unified Israel and conquered neighboring nations. He moved the capital from Hebron to Jerusalem. David was a general, a ruler, and a poet. The Book of Psalms from the Bible is attributed to him.

Dawn (English) or **Ushas** (Sanskrit: उषा dawn) Daughter of Dyaus (sky god). Her consort is the sun. The ever youthful Dawn appears as a young woman with uncovered breasts and rides in a splendid chariot, drawn by seven ruddy cows, which pushes back the darkness.

Djed Pillar (Egyptian: 𓊽𓏤) A prehistoric fetish, possibly a tree or pole with notches, which is a symbol of fertility, of grain, and also of Osiris, the god of vegetation. It is raised up at the end of the harvest. The ritual of the king raising the *djed* pillar is connected to maintaining the stability in the kingdom. It is also regarded as Osiris' backbone. Djedu, the name of the city of the oldest cult center of Osiris, is homophonic with the words for stability and endurance.

Dumuzi (Sumerian: 𒌉 𒍣 good child) The legendary ruler of Badtibira. Son of Enki and Sirtur. Lover and husband of Inanna. Dumuzi was a shepherd and later a king who was associated with the "sacred marriage rites" and the mourning rites; in later times, he was worshiped as Tammuz.

Echo (Greek: Ἠχώ echo) The daughter of the nymph Gaia, she is deprived of speech by the jealous Hera and wastes away when Narcissus does not return her love.

Ein-Gedi (Hebrew: עין גדי spring of the kid) A village on the west shore of the Dead Sea, famous for its spring and its vineyards.

Eleusis (Greek: Ἐλευσις) A sacred site near Athens where rites to Demeter were celebrated in the autumn. Performance of the sacred mysteries renewed the fertility of the earth and assured immortality to the initiates.

Enki (Sumerian: 𒀭 𒂗 𒆠 lord earth, subterranean regions; Akkadian: god of waters) The god of wisdom, waters, primeval regions, god of incantations. Son of An and Nammu. His consorts include Sirtur, Damgalnunna (floodwave), Ninhursag (lady of the mountain). In his human form, he is depicted seated on a throne in a temple holding a vessel from which two streams of water, the Tigris and the Euphrates, flow. In his animal form, he has a goat head and a fish body. A trickster and sometimes drunkard and womanizer, he is flexible, excitable, and restores stability, using craft and cunning rather than force. Beneficent, he offers counsel and advice to gods and humans and takes the side of humankind. The skillful originator of culture and order, he promotes fertility and builds temples. A mysterious god who guards and knows the powers of the *me,* as well as the way into and out of the underworld. His epithets include King of the Abzu, Master of the Ear, Understanding, Knowing One. *See* Abzu, Eridu.

Enlil (Sumerian: 𒀭𒂗𒆤 lord wind) King of the gods. Son of An and Ki. His union with Ninhursag brings the seasons and yearly flooding of the Tigris. His other consort is Ninlil. During the first month of the year, which is sacred to An and Enlil, the destinies of the gods and mortals are determined by An and Enlil and carried out by Enlil. The tablets of destiny belong to Enlil. The gods make yearly journeys to Nippur, Enlil's city, to receive Enlil's blessings for their cities and vegetation.

Ereshkigal (Sumerian: 𒀭𒊩𒆠𒃲 queen of the great earth) Queen of the underworld, darkness, death, and decay. Daughter of An. Her consorts are Gugalanna, then Ninazu, then Nergal (god of pestilence and fertility). In an Akkadian myth, Nergal is sent by the gods to the underworld because of his disrespect for Ereshkigal's messenger, Namtar (fate). Nergal seizes her hair and she succumbs, offering him her dominion, whereupon they become passionate lovers.

Eridu The ancient city of Eridu was located in southeastern Iraq. It was founded near the Persian Gulf, where the fresh and salt waters met. It was later situated 120 miles northwest of the Gulf. This earliest of ancient Sumerian city-states dates back to the eighth millenium B.C.E. and was mentioned throughout Mesopotamian history because of its antiquity and its relationship to Enki, the god of wisdom. *See* Abzu.

Eros (Greek: Ἔρως Love) (Latin: *Amor* = love, *Cupidus* = love) God of love. At the beginning of time, Eros was born with Ge (Earth), Tartarus, and Chaos. Later traditions say that he was the son of Aphrodite (and Ares or Hephaestus). He appears as a young archer with gold- and lead-tipped arrows, whose powers cause both gods and mortals to fall in love.

First Hill The manifestation of the emergence of the world. Atum is known as the First Hill. The early stepped mounds and the later pyramid form of tombs were likely to have been based on the First Hill. *See* Atum.

Galatur (Sumerian: priestly singer, young) An apprentice lamentation-priest.

Galla (Sumerian: "policemen") Creatures from the underworld. Wardens of heaven and earth, they are implacable servants of the underworld.

Ganymede (Greek: Γανυμήδης) Cupbearer to Jupiter. Because of his beauty, the son of Tros (King of Troy) was abducted by Jupiter to Olympus, where he became Jupiter's cupbearer.

Geb (Egyptian:) The earth god. Son of Shu and Tefnut. His consort is Nut. He appears as a goose, as a man holding a goose, and as a man lying under the body of Nut. After Shu withdrew from the earth, Geb raped his mother, Tefnut. Geb appointed Osiris as the first king. His epithets include Heir of the Gods, the Great Cackler.

Geshtinanna (Sumerian: grape of heaven) The lady of the grapevine. Daughter of Ningikugu and Enki. Her consort is Ningizzida (of the faithful tree). She belongs to the realm of the underworld.

Gilgamesh (Sumerian: 𒀭𒄑𒂵𒈩) The legendary ruler of Uruk (c. 2700–2500 B.C.E.). By some accounts, Gilgamesh is the son of the hero Lugalbanda and the goddess Ninsun. He appears on the Sumerian King List as the king of Uruk. In the Akkadian *Epic of Gilgamesh,* he is known for his courage, loyalty, and lust, for his encounter with death, and for his conflict with Inanna-Ishtar.

Graces (Greek: χάριτες graces) Three sisters from heaven who are the daughters of Zeus: *Aglaia* (Splendor), *Thalia* (Pleasure), *Euphrosyne* (Joy). Associated with Aphrodite, their aspects are charm, grace, and beauty.

Hathor (Egyptian: 𓉡𓁥 house with falcon) The cow goddess, the sky goddess, the goddess of love, beauty, dance, music, and drink. She appears as a great cow straddling the heavens, as a woman with horns, and as a woman with the sun-disk suspended between her horns and cow-ears. As the goddess Sekmet (power), she is destructive and devouring. In Hathor's rites, the king often dances before her; wine and beer are her sacred offerings. Her epithets include Eye of the Sun God, Re, the Beautiful One, the Golden One.

Heliopolis The city that was built on the First Hill. It is the ancient center of worship of the Sun God Re, in Lower Egypt. *See* First Hill.

Heshbon (Hebrew: חשבון) A city of northern Moab considered to be the inheritance of Gad, one of Jacob's sons.

Horus (Egyptian: 𓅃𓀭 falcon) King of Upper and Lower Egypt. Son of Osiris and Isis. He appears as a falcon and as a child (Harpocrates) with sidelocks and with a finger in his mouth. In early texts, Horus is thought of as a sky god, in the image of a falcon with outstretched wings, whose right eye is the sun and left eye is the moon. In these early texts, he is known as Horus the Elder and is the brother of Seth. *See* Seth.

Hours (Greek: Ὧραι seasons) The goddesses of the three seasons, and ministers to the gods. The daughters of Zeus and Themis are *Eunomia* (Good Government), *Dike* (Right), *Eirene* (Peace).

Huluppu (Sumerian: [cuneiform]) An unidentified tree in Sumer, possibly a willow or an oak. One of the trees imported from the east.

Inanna (Sumerian: 𒀭𒈹 queen of heaven) The great goddess. Daughter of Ningal and Nanna, she is also the daughter of An, who raised her to be his consort, the queen of heaven; also the consort of kings of Uruk, including Dumuzi. The rites connected to her date clusters and storehouses became known as "sacred marriage rites." Later Inanna was worshiped as the vegetation goddess, the goddess of love, the lady of the morning and evening stars (identified with the planet Venus), the lady of battle, and the hierodule. As goddess of the sheepfold, she is connected to thunderstorms and the lion-headed thunderbird. Her dance is the movement of battle lines; the thunderous sound of war chariots signifies her approach. Her emblems include the rosette, the lion, the sheepfold, and the gatepost with streamers.

Isis (Egyptian: 𓊨𓏏𓁐 seat, throne) The protective mortuary goddess and later, the goddess of healing. Daughter of Nut and Geb. Her consort is Osiris. Isis appears as a kite (a bird of prey) and as a woman with arms or wings around Osiris. She is often shown standing at the foot of the coffin. Her epithets include Goddess of Many Names, Eye of Re, The Great Magician, Egg of the Goose.

Jerusalem (Hebrew: ירושלם city of peace, city of Shalim, Canaanite god of dusk) The religious capital of Israel since the time of David. *See* David.

Juno (Latin) or Hera (Greek: Ἥρα) The goddess of marriage and childbirth. Her consort is Jupiter. As Juno Lucina (Latin: *lux* light), she cares for children from womb to light; as Juno Sororia (*soror* sister), she cares for girls at puberty; as Juno Zygia (*zygia* yoked), she guards the sanctity of marriage.

Jupiter (Latin) or Zeus (Greek: Ζεύς the shining father) Lord of the sky, ruler of gods and mortals. Son of Cronus and Rhea. Although his wife is Juno, he has many lovers, divine and mortal. He appears carrying a scepter with his emblems of power, a thunderbolt and an eagle. He is saved by his mother from being devoured by his father and grows up to depose Cronus.

Ka (Egyptian: 𓂓 raised hands) Each person is born with a ka, a double, a creative, preserving life force. When a person dies, the ka continues to live. When a person goes to ka, that person goes to his or her death or divine source. Ka is homophonic with the word "bull."

Kali (Sanskrit: काल time, blackness) A form of the mother goddess. Her consort is Shiva. She appears as a many-armed, black, bare-breasted, hungry crone, who is adorned with garlands of skulls and severed heads. She holds a noose, an iron hook, and a prayer book. She devours everything that lives in time and is rejuvenated by blood sacrifices.

Kama (Sanskrit: काम desire) The god of sexual and romantic love. Kama was self-born from the heart of Brahma or from the primeval waters. His consort is Rati. He appears with many arms, carrying a bowstring made of bees and five arrows made of flowers. He is attended by heavenly dancers, essences, and fragrances. When Kama is appeased, he can free the mind from desire. His epithet is Manmatha (he who churns the mind).

Kedar (Hebrew: כדר dark) A group of Arab herdsmen who dwelt in the eastern desert in darkly colored tents.

Khepri (Egyptian: 𓆣𓂋𓏏 beetle) Khepri is the manifestation of the Sun God at dawn. He appears as a human with a khepreer beetle head. The khepreer beetle (also called the scarab beetle) buries its eggs in the sand. Its offspring appear fully formed, suggesting autogenerative qualities. This idea was further reinforced by the dung that the beetles push, which was thought to contain their eggs.

King Arthur (Celtic) Arthur supposedly lived in fifth or sixth C.E. as a British king; in Welsh Chronicles he engaged in wars and hunts; in other legends he is depicted as wise, indecisive, and peace seeking. He established the Round Table to insure harmony and equality.

Kurgarra (Sumerian: 𒆳𒃻𒊏 place in the mountain) An actor or performer of cultic games, plays, dances, and music. He is often mentioned in connection with Inanna-Ishtar.

Lady of the Crown (Egyptian: 𓇅𓇋𓇋𓏏𓆗 Wadjet) The serpent goddess, Wadjet, the Uraeus. Wadjet is the goddess of Buto in the Delta whose sacred animal is the cobra. As a cobra, or fire-spitting animal, Wadjet became associated with the Eye of Re and the royal uraeus crown. In the middle of his forehead the king wore a serpent or royal cobra which had powers to protect him from evil by spitting fire. Wadjet was the goddess of Lower Egypt; the papyrus was supposed to have emerged from her body. Her name means "green one" and embodies the forces of growth.

Lakshmi (Sanskrit: लक्ष्मी she who has auspicious marks) The goddess of material prosperity, good fortune, and beauty. In one legend, her father the sage Bhrigu curses the gods; Lakshmi flees into the primeval waters where she is reborn during the churning of the Milky Ocean and emerges full-born and radiant, floating on a lotus. Vishnu immediately reaches for her and makes her his wife. She appears with four arms, one hand holds a lotus. Her incarnations as Vishnu's wife include Padma (Lotus-lady), Sita (Furrow), Dharani (Earth). Her epithets include Jewel, Goddess Beyond Reach, Powerful One, Ocean Born, Fickle-One, Mother of the World.

Lilith (Sumerian: the ghost maid) The name Lilith is derived from Sumerian and Akkadian references to malefic powers which were connected with uninhabited places. In later times, the name refers to a specific female deity, who appears as a nude winged goddess with a crown of horns and with animals under her taloned bird-feet.

Lingam (Sanskrit: लिङ्गम् sign) The symbol of Shiva's essence—an ever-erect potent phallus full of seed—is associated with the transformation of erotic energy into spiritual energy.

Lucina (Latin) Epithet of Juno as Patroness of Childbirth. *See* Juno.

Lulal (Sumerian: 𒇻 𒇲 honeyman) Demon-fighter. Son of An and Inanna. Connected to the water scorpion.

Lydia (Latin) An area of Asia Minor whose most famous king, Croesus, is said to have invented money. This is also the name of one of the seven Greek musical modes.

Maya (Sanskrit: माया measure out) Her consort is Vishnu. According to Vedic sources, she is the source of the visible universe and the manifestation of the creative mind. According to the Upanishads, she is the transformation of the absolute into material reality or the emanation of the phenomenal universe. Other interpretations of Maya are the illusion of material reality, the cosmic flux, deception.

The *Me* (Sumerian: 𒈨) Although essentially undefinable, the *me* are thought to be the powers, duties, and standards of the universe, both positive and negative, that have to be obeyed by gods and mortals. Enki received the *me* from Enlil's shrine (the Ekur) in Nippur, and kept them in his Abzu. Inanna won the *me* from Enki in a drinking bout and brought them back to her city's shrine in Uruk. At least 94 identifiable *me* are described in Sumerian texts. *See* Abzu.

Mecca (Arabic: مكة) Located in southwestern Arabia, the site of the holiest shrine in Islam is the Ká'ba. Its black stone, embedded in one corner, is said to be a meteorite which was found in the sands near Mecca. According to Muslim tradition, Abraham and his son Ishmael built the Ká'ba as a recreation of the heavenly temple.

Menaka (Sanskrit: मेनका) A demi-goddess, one of three *apsaras* (water nymphs) who seduces gods and mortals.

Mercury (Latin) or Hermes (Greek: Ἑρμῆς) Messenger of the gods. Son of Jupiter. He has many lovers, including Venus. He appears as a handsome young man with a winged helmet, carrying a caduceus. He was also worshiped in the form of a herm, a head on a square pillar with male genitals. In Greek myth, he stole cattle from his brother Apollo, and then gave Apollo the first lyre, which was made from a tortoise shell and the guts of the cattle. In return, Apollo gave Hermes the caduceus. His epithets include Protector of Travelers, Guardian of Flocks, Conductor of Souls to the Underworld, Conductor of Dreams, Trickster, Patron of Thieves.

Miletus (Greek: Μίλητος) A Greek city in Asia Minor near which an Oracle of Apollo is located.

Mount Carmel (Hebrew: הר כרמל) Mountain on the shore of the Mediterranean known for its beauty and fertility.

Mount Gilead (Hebrew: הר גלעד) The mountain on the east side of northern Jordan.

Muses (Greek: Μοῦσαθ) The patronesses of memory. The nine daughters of Menemosyne (memory) and Zeus are Clio, Euterpe, Thalia, Melpomene, Terpsichore, Erato, Polymnia, Urania, Calliope. They lived on Mount Helicon.

Nanna (Sumerian: 𒀭𒋀𒆠 moon) Moon god. Son of Enlil and Ninlil. He was born when Enlil raped Ninlil, forcing open her too small vagina. His consort is Ningal. As Nanna, he is the full moon; as Suen he is the sickle moon. Sometimes he is depicted riding in a boat, which is the sickle moon. He appears in his bull form as a herder who drives the stars across the pasture of heaven. His cities, Ur and Harran (in western Mesopotamia), were both associated with the patriarch Abraham.

Neith (Egyptian: 𓈖𓏏𓋋𓁐) Oldest goddess, creator, great mother, warrior goddess, protective goddess. Neith appears as a woman wearing the the Red Crown of Lower Egypt. Her emblems include a shield with crossed arrows and two bows. Mother of mothers and the father of fathers, she is thought to be two-thirds male and one-third female. She is connected to the primordial flood. Neith created the first gods and prophesied the birth of the Sun God. A protector of royalty as well as humankind, she was worshiped at Sais in the Lower Delta. Her name is homophonic with *Net*, the word for crown.

Nemesis (Greek: Νέμεσις deal out, dispense) Goddess of retribution and measure. The daughter of Nyx (night), she protects gods from encroachment by mortals. She distributes justice and punishes pride and secret vices.

Nephthys (Egyptian: 𓎟𓏏𓉗𓏏𓁐 house with lord/lady) A mortuary goddess, responsible for the care of the dead. Daughter of Nut and Geb. Her consort is Seth. She appears as a kite (a bird of prey) and as a woman with outstretched arms and wings caring for Osiris. She stands at the head of the coffin.

Nereus (Greek: Νηρεύς) Sea god. Son of Pontus and Gaia. With his consort Doris (daughter of Oceanus), Nereus had fifty daughters, the Nereids, who spun, sang, and danced on the sea. He appears as an old man of the sea, with a long flowing beard and hair crowned with seaweed.

Ningal (Sumerian: 𒀭𒊩𒌆𒃲 great queen, lady) Daughter of Nigikuga (lady of the reed) and Enki. Her consort is Nanna.

Ninshubur (Sumerian: 𒀭𒊩𒌆𒋚) Early goddess of Uruk. Special messenger and devoted servant of Inanna, also messenger and servant of An. According to one hymn, she is the wife of Nergal. When serving An, the identity of Ninshubur is male.

Nippur (Sumerian: 𒂗𒆤𒆠) An ancient Sumerian city-state in southeastern Iraq that is located 90 miles southeast of Babylon. Although not politically powerful, the numerous literary clay tablets excavated from Nippur reflect the city's role as the leading intellectual and religious center of ancient Mesopotamia. It was Enlil's city. *See* Enlil.

Nun (Egyptian: 𓏌𓏌𓏌𓈗𓀭) The father of the gods; the primeval waters; the place of creation.

Nut (Egyptian: 𓏏𓈗𓁐) A sky goddess, the personification of the sky, a mortuary goddess, the Coffin. Daughter of Tefnut and Shu. Her consort is Geb; her lover, Thoth. She appears as a woman with a waterpot on her head and as a woman with a long blue dress whose body arcs from horizon to horizon and contains all the heavenly bodies. She is the mother of Re and gives birth to him each dawn. Sometimes depicted as a cow goddess, Nut is also associated with Hathor.

Nymphs (Greek: νύμφη bride, young marriageable woman) The spirits of the Greek countryside who inhabit and animate hills, streams, and forests.

Oracle of Apollo (Greek: Ἀπόλλων) Divine revelations were given at Apollo's temples, which are located at Delphi and at Didyma near Miletus. They offered answers to those who came with a pure heart. The answers preserved and promoted religious, political, and social institutions.

Osiris (Egyptian: 𓊨𓁹𓀭 eye over a throne) King of the dead, the judge in the Hall of Judgment, and the vegetation god. Son of Geb and Nut. His consort is Isis, his sister. Osiris appears as a green-, white-, or black-faced, bearded man, carrying a staff and flail. He wears a tight, white garment and the Atef crown, which is a combination of the Double Crown and the White Crown with a solar disk on the tip. He is associated with Tammuz and other vegetation gods who die each year; however, Osiris never returns to earth, he lives forever in the underworld. Every deceased hoped to become Osiris in the mortuary realm and be reborn into eternal life. His epithets include the Eternally Good One, the Perfect One.

Palaemon (Greek: Παλαίμων wrestler) Sea God. Son of Ino. He befriends the shipwrecked.

Pan (Greek: Πάν) Pastoral god. Son of Hermes and a nymph. His upper part is human and his lower part is goatlike. He plays a seven-reeded pipe. With his shaggy beard and horns, he is uncouth, lascivious, and prone to having amorous adventures with nymphs and peasants. He was worshiped by shepherds.

Paphos (Greek: Πάφος) The chief center of Venus' cult on Cyprus.

Parvati (Sanskrit: पार्वती mountain girl) The lady of the mountain. Daughter of Menaka (intellect) and Himavat (the snowy mountain), she is the conscious element of the universe. Her consort is Shiva. Born dark complexioned, through the heat of her penances she became fair-skinned and willfully drew

Shiva's attention to her. Once, when she playfully covered Shiva's eyes, the world was thrown into darkness. Shiva then grew a third eye in his forehead. The third eye could shoot fire, destroying Shiva's enemies. Parvati and Shiva engage in endless lovemaking as well as quarrels. One of their embraces was so passionate, that they became one being. In Hindu temples, they are represented as the yoni and the lingam. Parvati is a mortal form of the Universal Mother (Durga, Kali . . .). *See* Shiva.

Pluto (Latin) or Hades (Greek: Πλοῦτος wealth) God of the underworld, death, fertility, and wealth. Son of Cronus and Rhea. His consort is Proserpina. In Greek myth, he takes Persephone by force knowing that her mother Demeter will never willingly consent to her departure.

Portunus (Latin) A god who protects harbors.

Proserpine (Latin) or Persephone (Greek: Περσεφόνη) The queen of the underworld who presides over the rites of the dead. Daughter of Ceres and Jupiter. She appears as a young virgin. In the Greek myth, she was abducted by Hades to the underworld when she was picking the narcissus flower. Her mother Demeter vowed to ravage the earth if Persephone was not released. She was released but forced to remain in the underworld one-third of the year because she ate seeds when in Hades' house. Hades became her husband.

Psyche (Greek: ψυχή soul, butterfly) The story of Psyche and Eros is known only from Apuleius' *The Golden Ass,* books 4 and 5.

Puranas (Sanskrit: पुराण old) A collection of noncanonical texts that include stories about the gods, the interaction of gods and mortals, cosmology, cosmogony, and the philosophical implications of the stories and their teachings. They were written between the seventh and twelfth centuries C.E.

Pythia (Greek: Πυθία inquire) A priestess of Apollo. At ritual times the pythia bathes, eats herbs, sits on a tripod in the temple sanctuary, falls into a trance, and utters inchoate words that are interpreted by the surrounding priests. She is bound to the laws of chastity and temperance.

Qays (Arabic: قيس) Identified with the poet Qays ibn al-Mulawwah, who lived in the second half of seventh century C.E.

Rati (Sanskrit: रति lust) Daughter of Daksha. Her consort is Kama.

Re (Egyptian: 𓂋𓏤𓇳𓏤𓀭 sun) The manifestation of the Sun God at noon. Re first appears in Nun, the place of creation, as a child on a fragrant blue water lily. By means of his word, Re creates the gods from his sweat and humanity from his tears. He rules with his daughter, Maat, the Feather of Truth, who is the personification of truth and divinely appointed order.

Salacia (Latin=leap) The goddess of water who makes waters spring up from ground. She is associated with Neptune.

Saraswati (Sanskrit: सरस्वती lake, ownership) The goddess of learning, wisdom, speech, eloquence, and the patroness of the arts and music. Born from Brahma's mind, she becomes Brahma's wife. In an early legend, she is the personification of the River, Saraswat. She is the source of creation by word. Depicted as a graceful woman with four arms and a crescent moon on her forehead, she is dressed in white and sits on a swan and carries a vina, a book, and a lotus. Her epithets include Speech, Mother of the Vedas. *See* Brahma.

Sati (Sanskrit: सती to be, to be true) Daughter of Virani (profundity) and Daksha (Ritual-Skill). Her consort is Shiva.

Sayyid (Arabic: سيّد) A descendant of the prophet Mohammed; an honorific for master or lord.

Seth (Egyptian: 𓃩) The god associated with storms, the desert, the wind, and disorder. Son of Geb and Nut. His consort in the early times is Nephthys; later consorts are Anath and Astarte. Seth appears as a greyhound with an upright tail, ears, and almond-shaped eyes. He also appears as a man. Seth is associated with the pig, the wild boar, and the hippopotamus. In early texts the two brothers, Horus the Elder and Seth, battle. Horus the Elder rips out Seth's testicles; Seth rips out Horus' left eye, which is the moon. *See* Horus.

Shades (Greek: έιδωλα shadows, little forms) The dead who have no body or consciousness.

Shakti (Sanskrit: शक्ति to be able, to be possible) The divine energy of the universe, the power of manifestation, the female organ, material power.

Shiva (Sanskrit: शिव benign) In the trinity of gods, the Destroyer. Among others, his consorts include Sati and later Parvati. As a demon slayer, Shiva's supreme power lies in his yogic austerities and purity. His earlier form as Rudra, the Vedic god of storms and lightning, reflects his fertile, erotic powers. He is depicted with one or five faces, four arms, three eyes, and a blue throat. His two upper hands hold a drum and a flame; the lower hands are in gestures of protection and action. In some representations, he carries a drum, a human skull, a horn, the bow Pinaka and his lightning trident. He is decorated with snakes and wears a necklace of skulls and a tiger skin. In his red hair are the crescent-shaped moon and the Ganges river. He rides on Nandi, his white bull. He is associated with the genital center, meditation, sleep, the foliage of a tree, the lingam. His epithets include Lord of the Dance, Lord of Beasts.

Shu (Egyptian: 𓆄𓅱𓀭) The god of air and life. Son of Atum, he was created from Atum's spit and semen. His consort is Tefnut. He appears as a lion, as a man with a feather on his head, and as a man who stands on Geb and supports Nut, thereby separating the two.

Shulamite (Hebrew: שולמית woman from shulam, woman of peace, well-being, perfection) A resident of Shulam, a city in northern Israel.

Siren (Greek: Σειρήν) One of three water nymphs who, by their singing, lure sailors to their graves. They live between Circe's Island and Scylla.

Solomon (Hebrew: שלמה peace, well-being) The king of Israel in the tenth century B.C.E. Son of David and Bathsheba, he is reported to have had over 700 wives from many lands. He generated international commerce in Jerusalem and built a splendid palace and temple. He is known for his wisdom, understanding, poetry, and singing. Books from the Bible that are attributed to him are The Song of Songs, Ecclesiastes, and Proverbs.

Styx (Greek: Στύξ from hate) A river in the underworld that flowed around the House of Hades nine times. Waters from the high vaulted rock trickle down into the River Styx. The gods swear an inviolable oath by the River Styx, which cannot be dissolved.

Sunboat There are two sunboats, a morning boat and an evening boat. They carry the gods through the heavens and the underworld. In the Sunboat of Morning, Re is the leader of the gods. In the Sunboat of Evening, Thoth, as the moon, leads the gods. Seth sits at the bow of the Sunboat to fend off Apopis, the great sun-devouring serpent.

Taenarus (Greek: Ταίναρος) A promontory in southern Peloponnesus, where the entrance to Pluto's dominion was thought to exist.

Tartarus (Greek: Τάρταρος) The region below the House of Hades, which was a place of eternal darkness where the damned are tormented.

Tefnut (Egyptian:) The goddess of moisture and order. Daughter of Atum, created from Atum's spit and semen. Her consort is Geb. She is depicted with the face of a lion or as a woman with a sun's disk encircled by a cobra on her head. In an early myth, Tefnut, estranged from Re, flees to Nubia where she becomes a lioness and drinks and feeds on human and animal flesh. Thoth and Shu entice her back to Egypt with music and drink. Hathor replaces Tefnut in certain versions of the same story. Maat also replaces Tefnut as order and truth.

Thoth (Egyptian: ibis) The god of justice, the moon, and time. He is the scribe of the gods and the recorder in the Hall of Judgment. He appears as a man with an ibis head holding a palette with a reed pen. He also appears as a baboon. When the deceased appears before Osiris in the Hall of Judgment and his fate is weighed by placing the Feather of Truth on one side of the scale and his heart on the other, Thoth registers the verdict. Anubis adjusts the balance. *See* Anubis, Osiris.

Tintagel (Celtic) Located on the North Cornish coast, supposedly the castle where Arthur was conceived.

Tirzah (Hebrew: תרצה pleasantness, grace) A valley region in central Israel belonging to the clan of Tirzah, who sought justice from Moses. Tirzah became the first capital of the northern kingdom.

Two Lands (Egyptian:) Upper Egypt is located in the southern part of Egypt. The kings of Upper Egypt wore the White (the reed crown) and were associated with the Nekhbet or the Vulture Goddess, whose city, Nekheb, dates back to 6000 B.C.E. Lower Egypt, whose center is in the Delta, is located in the north. The kings of Lower Egypt wore the papyrus Red Crown (known as the *Net*) and were associated with Wadjet, the cobra goddess, and the bee. The kings of the Two Lands wore the Double Crown, consisting of two ostrich feathers, which was a combination of the White, the crown of Upper Egypt, and the Red Crown of Lower Egypt. By wearing the crown, the kings had access to the powers of the goddesses who were connected to the crowns. *See* Neith, Hathor, Lady of the Crown.

Tyet Knot (Egyptian:) A symbol of Isis, Isis' girdle, a popular protective amulet. Made of cloth or leather, it is similar in form to the ankh except its horizontal arms droop downwards. The *tyet* is a symbol of hidden forces of germination connected to creation. It was often combined with the *djed* symbol of Osiris in temple decorations.

Ur (Sumerian:) One of the earliest Sumerian city-states. It was located on the former channel of the Euphrates River in southeastern Iraq. The numerous clay tablets excavated from Ur (of administrative documents, temple hymns, and building inscriptions) reveal its importance as a great political and economic center of southern Mesopotamia. It is the site of royal tombs and the city of Nanna. In the Bible it is referred to as Ur of the Chaldees; the modern-day name is Muqaiyar. *See* Nanna.

Uruk (Sumerian:) Uruk is located 150 miles southeast of Baghdad and 12 miles from the Euphrates. Excavation of the remains of this earliest urban city (dating from 3500 to 2900 B.C.E.) reveals its sophisticated temple architecture, the first writing on clay tablets, and its refined and detailed art—temple vases, bas-reliefs, musical instruments, and jewelry. The oldest preserved temple in Uruk, the Eanna (the house of heaven), was built of brightly colored, dried bricks to honor the city's goddess, Inanna. The biblical name of Uruk was Erech; the modern-day name is Warka.

Utu (Sumerian: 𒀭𒌓 sun) The sun god, god of justice and oracles. Son of Nanna and Ningal. His consort is Ninkarra (lady of the dark). He maintains law, punishes evil, utters oracles, and helps widows and orphans. Whether on earth during the day or in the underworld at night, he is present wherever justice is being carried out. He is a powerful warrior and fights evil. He carries a saw and is portrayed rising between two mountain peaks.

Vedas (Sanskrit: वेद knowledge) A canonical collection of hymns, myths, incantations, poetic reflections, and prayers, compiled by the ancient seers. Practicing Hindus believe that the proper recitation of the Vedas brings sacred power to both teacher and listener. Modern scholars claim that the Vedas were composed between 1000 B.C.E. and 700 B.C.E.

Venus (Latin) or Aphrodite (Greek: Ἀφροδίτη) The goddess of love and beauty was self-born from the *aphros* (sea-foam) which was floating near Uranus' severed genitals. Other traditions claim she was the daughter of Dione and Jupiter. Although her husband is Vulcan, her many lovers include Mars and Adonis. She is characteristically spiteful, benevolent, beautiful, and filled with sexual passion. She is identified with a variety of Near Eastern goddesses of fertility, including Astarte, Ishtar, Inanna.

Vijaya (Sanskrit: विजय victory, hemp) A minor goddess. Sister of Sati.

Vishnu (Sanskrit: विष्णु penetrate, pervade) In the trinity of gods, the Preserver. He often appears on a lotus with his consort, Lakshmi. Vishnu measured the universe with three steps, considered by some to be the dawn, noon, and sunset, and by others, the earth, atmosphere, and sky. He appears dark-complexioned, sleeping on a coiled serpent, and dressed in royal robes. In his four hands he holds a conch, a discus, a club, and a lotus. He carries Sarnga, his bow, and rides on Garuda, who is half-eagle and half-human. He is associated with the navel, the dreamlike state, the trunk of a tree. He is the source of continuity, cohesion, light, life, and transcendence. He is also the intermediary between the deities and mortals. His incarnations include the fish, tortoise, boar, dwarf, Rama, Krishna, Buddha. In his mortal incarnations, Vishnu guards the righteous, destroys evil, and protects the *dharma,* the law. Among his 1,008 epithets are Lord of Waters.

Vulcan (Latin) or Hephaestos (Greek: Ἥφαιστος) God of fire and the forge. Son of Jupiter and Juno. His consort is Venus. He appears as an ugly, deformed cripple, with a long beard and a small cap on his head. He carries a hammer, a pincers, and a thunderbolt. In Greek myth, Hephaestus is flung by Hera from Olympus because of his deformity; his first crafted work is a golden throne that entraps Hera. He creates sublime works of art from metal.

Zephyrus (Greek: Ζέφυρος) West Wind. Son of Eos (dawn) and Astrus (starry).

Zion (Hebrew: ציון parched hill or designated place) The name of the hill that David conquered and designated for the temple, the permanent abode of God in the biblical period.

Zygia (Latin from Greek: ζύγια of the yoke) Epithet of Juno as Patroness of Marriage. *See* Juno.

Books Consulted for the Glossary

Danielou, Alain. *Gods of India.* New York: Inner Traditions, 1985.

Dictionary of the Middle Ages. New York: American Council of Learned Societies, 1989.

Dwight, M. A. *Grecian and Roman Mythology.* New York: Putnam's, 1849.

Eliade, Mircea. *The Encyclopedia of Religion.* New York: Macmillan, 1987.

Ions, Veronica. *Indian Mythology.* New York: P. Bedrick, 1984.

Lacy, Norris, J. *The Arthurian Encyclopedia.* New York: Garland Press, 1986.

Lurker, Manfred. *The Gods and Symbols of Ancient Egypt.* New York: Thames & Hudson, 1980.

Rundle Clark, R. T. *Myth and Symbol in Ancient Egypt.* London: Thames & Hudson, 1959.

Walker, Benjamin. *The Hindu World,* vols. 1 and 2. New York: Praeger, 1968.

Watterson, Barbara. *The Gods of Ancient Egypt.* New York: Facts on File, 1984.

FOLKLORE NOTES

ISIS AND OSIRIS

There is no extant Egyptian text called "Isis and Osiris." I have composed the story by choosing from a large corpus of Egyptian and Greek texts. In addition, I have drawn from both sacred and secular texts. A great time span, over 2,000 years, separates the Pyramid texts, which date back to 2350 B.C.E., and Plutarch, who wrote in 120 C.E. Would that all the texts were Egyptian and from a 200-year period, but I have been grateful for whatever I have found and hope that further scholarship will bring further illuminations to the story.

Because this is the one story in the collection that is new and not available elsewhere, I am providing extensive notes on my sources for students of Egyptology, folklorists, and others who are interested in these texts. With few exceptions, I have not invented new material, but stood in awe of the Egyptians' powers of fantasy and imagination. My trip to Egypt in 1983 to see the shrines of the gods and goddesses reinforced that respect.

FOLKLORE NOTES

Sources:

Birth of the creator to the birth of the gods:

Bremner-Rhind Papyrus IV, "D. The Book of Overthrowing Apophis" (310 B.C.E.), translator R. O. Faulkner, *Journal of Egyptian Archaeology,* vol. 24. London: Egypt Exploration Society, 1938.

Atum, Shu, and Tefnut in the Nun:

Ancient Egyptian Pyramid Texts (Fifth Dynasty, 2350–2323 B.C.E.) Utterance 600, translator R. O. Faulkner. Warminister: Aris and Phillips, 1969.

The Ancient Egyptian Coffin Texts, vol. 1, Spell 80 (Middle Kingdom, 2040–1640 B.C.E.), translator R. O. Faulkner. Warminister: Aris and Phillips, 1973.

Osiris journeys abroad:

Diodorus Siculus, *The Library of History,* Book I, ch. 20–22 (49 B.C.E.), translator C. H. Oldfather. In *The Loeb Classical Library,* Cambridge, Mass.: Harvard University Press, 1969.

Plutarch, *Moralia V,* Isis and Osiris, ch. 13 (120 B.C.E.), translator Frank Cole Babbitt. In *The Loeb Classical Library,* Cambridge, Mass.: Harvard University Press, 1969.

Portrait of Isis:

Invention of Wolkstein.

Love poems:

Adapted from secular love poems in: Papyrus Chester Beatty I (Twentieth Dynasty, thirteenth to twelfth century B.C.E.), Papyrus Harris 500 (Eighteenth Dynasty, 1300 B.C.E.), and The Cairo Vase, (Nineteenth Dynasty, 1200 B.C.E.), translator Michael V. Fox. In *The Song of Songs and the Ancient Egyptian Love Songs,* Madison, Wis.: University of Madison Press, 1985. (N.B. There are no such love poems between Isis and Osiris.)

Seth's plotting and killing of Osiris:

Plutarch, *Moralia V,* Isis and Osiris, ch. 13 and 14 (120 B.C.E.), translator Frank Cole Babbitt. In *The Loeb Classical Library,* Cambridge, Mass.: Harvard University Press, 1969.

Seth tricks Nephthys:

Wolkstein's expansion.

Isis mourns Osiris:
Bremner-Rhind Papyrus I, "A. The Songs of Isis and Nephthys" (310 B.C.E.), translator R. O. Faulkner, *Journal of Egyptian Archaeology,* vol. 22, part II. London: Egypt Exploration Society, 1936.

Isis in Byblos, Isis cares for queen's child, Isis returns:
Plutarch, *Moralia V,* Isis and Osiris, ch. 14–17 (120 B.C.E.), translator Frank Cole Babbitt. In *The Loeb Classical Library,* Cambridge, Mass.: Harvard University Press, 1969.

Isis mourns Osiris on the boat:
Papyrus Berlin 3008, *Les Lamentations d'Isis and de Nephthys* (Ptolemaic, 300 B.C.E.), translator P. J. De Horrack. Paris: Librarie Tross, 1866.

Seth cuts up Horus' body:
Plutarch, *Moralia V,* Isis and Osiris, ch. 18 (120 B.C.E.), translator Frank Cole Babbitt. In *The Loeb Classical Library,* Cambridge, Mass.: Harvard University Press, 1969.

Isis cries to the gods:
The Ancient Egyptian Coffin Texts, vol. 1, Spell 148 (Middle Kingdom, 2040–1640 B.C.E.), translator R. O. Faulkner. Warminister: Aris and Phillips, 1973.

Isis and the woman of Buto, the birth of Horus, the sickness of Horus, the intervention of Thoth:
Metternich Stela, Spells 90 and 91 (350 B.C.E.), translator J. F. Borghouts. In *Ancient Egyptian Magical Texts,* Leiden: E. J. Brill, 1978.

Isis and the secret name of Re:
From two manuscripts: Papyrus Turin LXXVII plus XXXI: 1–5 (Lower Egypt, 1350–1200 B.C.E.) and Papyrus Chester Beatty XI: Hieratic Papyri in BM Series (Thebes, 1200 B.C.E.). In *Ancient Near Eastern Texts,* editor James Pritchard, translator John A. Wilson. Princeton: University of Princeton Press, 1955.

The Contendings of Horus and Seth:
Papyrus Chester Beatty I, Hieratic text (1200 B.C.E.), translator Miriam Lichtheim. *Ancient Egyptian Literature,* Vol. II: *The New Kingdom,* Berkeley: University of California Press, 1976.

Horus sends a message to Osiris in the underworld:
Ancient Egyptian Pyramid Texts, Utterance 482 (Fifth Dynasty,

2350–2323 B.C.E.), translator R. O. Faulkner. Warminister: Aris and Phillips, 1969.

Isis and Horus at High Hill; Isis places Re's name in Horus' heart: Wolkstein's expansion.

For consistency throughout the story I have used Khepri/Re/Atum instead of Ptah or Pre-Harakhti, and the Double Crown instead of the White crown.

INANNA AND DUMUZI

The story "Inanna and Dumuzi" is based on Sumerian love songs, poems, and stories deciphered by S. N. Kramer and other Sumerian scholars from the Sumerian cuneiform tablets dating back to around 2,000 B.C.E.

I have pieced together, arranged, and abbreviated the translations of these Sumerian fragments to form a coherent love story. In a few instances, I have added phrases to clarify the text. For folklore notes on the individual fragments and unabbreviated texts, see *Inanna, Queen of Heaven and Earth, Her Stories and Hymns from Sumer* by Diane Wolkstein and S. N. Kramer (New York: Harper & Row, 1983).

SHIVA AND SATI

The story "Shiva and Sati" is based on "The Sacrifice of Daksha" from Vedic sources, which date from 1000 to 700 B.C.E., and Shiva and Sati legends from the Puranas, which date from the fifth century to the twelfth century C.E.

My rendition is based on "Four Episodes from the Romance of the Goddess" from the book *The King and the Corpse* by Heinrich Zimmer, edited by Joseph Campbell (Princeton: Princeton University Press, Bollingen Series XI, 1973) and Diane Wolkstein's "The Eternal Dance of the Universe" in *Parabola,* vol. 5, no. 4, 1980.

THE SONG OF SONGS

The Hebrew love poetry of "The Song of Songs" is attributed to King Solomon and found in the Hebrew Masoretic text. Orthodox Jews and conservative Christians believe each word to be divinely inspired. Modern secular scholars consider the book to be a compilation of texts composed at various times between 900 and 300 B.C.E.

My rendition is a line-by-line translation from the Hebrew with the deletion of two and a half lines (Chapter 6, verses 5b–7). I have used pronouns to suggest the speakers and stanza breaks to suggest scene or mood changes. In a few instances, I have added words to amplify or specify the meaning.

No quotes are used to allow for the free flow of the text.

PSYCHE AND EROS

Psyche's womanly quest for love forms the central tale in *The Golden Ass,* a novel written by Apuleius in the second century C.E. in which the hero, Lucius, hears and experiences countless love tales in his own quest for divine love.

My telling is a translation based on Philip Shutz's literal translation from the Latin of Apuleius' fairy tale as found in *The Golden Ass.* I have used the Greek word *Eros* rather than the Latin word *Amor* because of its more evocative quality. I have also interwoven material from other sources to describe the rites of the Oracle of Apollo at Miletus.

LAYLA AND MAJNUN

In the twelfth century C.E., Shirvanshah Akhsetan, a Caucasian ruler, commissioned the elegant Persian poet Nizami to write a Persian romance based on Arabic folk legends, dating back to the seventh century C.E., of the mad poet Majnun and the beautiful Layla.

My version is based on two prose translations of this romance: Peter Chelkowski's *Mirror of the Invisible World* (New York: Metropolitan Museum of Art, 1975) and R. Gelpke's *The Story of Layla and Majnun* (Boulder, Colo.: Shambhala, 1978).

TRISTAN AND ISEULT

The legend of Tristan is of Celtic origin. Many versions were developed in Europe from the ninth to twelfth centuries C.E. and written down from the twelfth century on.

I have based my composition on the following sources: Alan S. Frederick's translation of *Beroul, The Romance of Tristan* (twelfth century C.E., Anglo-Norman), New York: Penguin, 1985; William Hatto's translation of Gottfried von Strassburg's *Tristan* (thirteenth century C.E., German), New York: Penguin, 1960; Paul Schach's translation of *The Saga of Tristan and Isond* (thirteenth century C.E., Norse), Lincoln, Neb.: University of Nebraska Press, 1973; and Joseph Bédier's translation of *The Romance of Tristan and Iseult* (nineteenth century C.E., French), New York: Vintage, 1965.

ACKNOWLEDGMENTS

My love and appreciation to:

Rachel Cloudstone Zucker who has known, lived with, and honored each of the stories.

Jinx Roosevelt, my dearest friend, who read and edited each story numerous times, was present at every major performance of the stories, and gently, but continuously, reminded me of the necessity of completing the book.

My friends who read the text with enthusiasm and discerning questions and comments: Victoria Fraser, Brooke Goffstein, Shirley Keller, Judith Kroll, Kaye Lindauer, Susan Thomas, Gary Wolkstein.

Barry Ulanov who encouraged me to dare the fool and whose fine insight gave perspective to each of the stories in the collection.

Phylis and Philip Morrison whose considered and lively listening shaped many of the stories.

Hugh Van Dusen whose sustained belief in the stories acted as a lighthouse over the years.

Geoffrey Gordon, an inspired musician, with whom I have shared many wonderful hours of rehearsals both on "Inanna and Dumuzi" and "The Song of Songs," and whose moving, subtle playing creates an atmosphere for us to experience that for which we have no words.

Kaye Lindauer of Syracuse University, Aryeh Maidenbaum, Director of the C. G. Jung Foundation of New York City, and Steve Curry, Director of the General Studies Program at New York University, who have all cared deeply for the stories and generously provided opportunities for their performances.

Stephanie Gunning of HarperCollins for her patience, editing, and unflaggingly cheerful support, Arne Lewis for his clear and caring advice for the design, Molly Friedrich, a wonderful agent, whose very voice lifts the spirit.

Benjamin Zucker who gave me the gift of *Mirror of the Invisible World,* containing "Layla and Majnun," Erlo Van Waveren who taught me much about myth, Irina Pabst whose inspiration and hard work helped to make Winter Tales by Candlelight a reality.

Wendy Heckler, a brilliant flautist and accompanist for "Tristan and Iseult," Elizabeth Williams and Joseph Forte whose lively conversations always placed myth in context, Charles Mee who encouraged me in the craft of writing.

Many thanks to the following scholars for their help with the texts:

ISIS AND OSIRIS:

Diane Guzman, reference librarian of the Wilbour Library, as well as the curators of the Egyptian Department of the Brooklyn Museum, for their patience and willingness over a period of four years to answer a beginner's endless questions. At the Wilbour Library I had the opportunity to read specifically as well as at random.

Professors Leonard Lesko and Barbara Lesko of Brown University who generously gave their time and guidance in helping me track down the many sources of the text.

Susan Tower Hollis of Scripps College who scrupulously read the text, helped clarify folklore references, and aided in the editing of the Egyptian section of the glossary. It is her hope, as well as that of all the other Egyptologists I worked with, that this rendering and the folklore notes will encourage those enamoured of the text to go back to the originals and work and play with them in greater depth.

INANNA AND DUMUZI:

Dr. Miguel Civil of the Oriental Institute (glossary), Dr. Tova Meltzer of Scripps College (glossary and cuneiform calligraphy).

SHIVA AND SATI:

Dr. Judith Kroll of the University of Texas at Austin (text and glossary), Dr. A. Bharati of Syracuse University (glossary), Dr. Wendy Doniger of University of Chicago (glossary), Mudit Tyagi (Sanskrit calligraphy).

THE SONG OF SONGS:

Dr. Ed Greenstein of the Jewish Theological Seminary (text and glossary), Dr. Ray Scheindlin of the Jewish Theological Seminary, Dr. Dan Ben-Amos of the University of Pennsylvania, Dr. Yosef Yerushalmi of Columbia University, Dr. Tova Meltzer of Scripps College (Hebrew calligraphy).

PSYCHE AND EROS:

Dr. Tamara Green of Hunter College (glossary, text, and Greek calligraphy) with added appreciation for her illuminating classes and lectures on Greek and Roman mythology.

LAYLA AND MAJNUN:

Dr. Peter Chelkowski of the Kevorkian Center for Middle Eastern Studies, New York University (text and glossary).

TRISTAN AND ISEULT:

Dr. Barry Ulanov, Professor Emeritus of Barnard, Dr. Joan Ferrante of Columbia University.

Thanks to:

The Virginia Colony for the Creative Arts, Bill Smith and the staff for four visits and the concentrated time and quiet to work on "Psyche and Eros" and "Tristan and Iseult."

Cummington Colony of the Arts for two visits and the concentrated time to work on "Isis and Osiris."

Doris Albrecht, reference librarian at the C. G. Jung Library in New York City, Todd Thompson, reference librarian at the New York City Public Library 42nd St. branch; who both suggested books before the asking.

And above all, my gratitude and love to:

The Creator for offering me this assignment.